Many modern pastors su ... of a biblical paradigm fo. ... . and the absence of the unique wisdom that comes from faithful pastoral mentors outside our present generation. You hold in your hands the remedy for them both. Jeremy Walker in his book *On the Side of God* brings to life the noteworthy character and ministry of the eighteenth century English Baptist, Andrew Fuller. As one of the most credible modern voices on Fuller, Walker writes with a clarity and precision that reminds us of why Andrew Fuller continues to be one of the most important voices for pastors in any generation. Pastors, read this book! You will be freshly challenged and inspired by the faithfulness of this man and his ministry.

—Brian Croft
Senior Pastor, Auburndale Baptist Church

We need the examples of godly men who have gone before us, who have served the Lord with faithfulness and excellence. This is precisely what we have in the noted English Baptist pastor-scholar Andrew Fuller. In this book, Jeremy Walker has done outstanding work to take us back to the eighteenth and nineteenth centuries, when Fuller was one of the key leaders of the Modern Missions Movement, and makes this seminal figure come alive. Read this book, walk in the footsteps of Fuller, and you will be greatly helped.

—Steven J. Lawson
President, OnePassion Ministries

In this brief work on the life of Andrew Fuller, Jeremy Walker has once again placed a great deal of treasure in a very small box. I cannot decide whether to call this book a biography, a devotional, or an instructional manual on practical ministry. It fits all three categories without a fault. I recommend this work to all without reservation and with the greatest expectation of benefit. It will place the aspiring minister on the right track and remind the seasoned minister of the true character and duty of a faithful steward of Christ.

—Paul David Washer
Founder, HeartCry Missionary Society

Fuller was essentially a man of the people pastoring a growing congregation in a market town in the English Midlands. He was not one of the famous preachers of the eighteenth century, but his faithful ministry deserves to be more widely known and understood. He has been misrepresented by some who seem never to have read his writings, while others who have admired his work, have completely failed to understand the strength of his Calvinism. Here we have an excellent introduction to Fuller's life and work. This is more than a biographical record; Walker has dug deeply into Fuller's pastoral writings and it becomes evident that Fuller has ministered to his own soul and strengthened his desires to be a faithful servant to Jesus Christ. Andrew Fuller may at first appear an austere character, but the reader soon discovers his heart of gold and deep love for Christ and his gospel. This is a challenging book; I warmly recommend it.

—Robert W. Oliver
Pastor, Old Baptist Church in Bradford-on-Avon

ON THE
SIDE OF
GOD

THE LIFE
AND LABORS
of
ANDREW
FULLER

ON THE
SIDE OF
GOD

THE LIFE
AND LABORS
of
ANDREW
FULLER

JEREMY
WALKER

FREE GRACE PRESS

On the Side of God:
The Life and Labors of Andrew Fuller (1754–1815)

Published by Free Grace Press
1076 Harkrider
Conway, AR 72032
freegracepress.com

Cover design by Scott Schaller
Scottschallerdesigns.com

Cover portrait provided by Norman Hopkins

ISBN: 978-1-59925-606-1

For the brothers of

"The Gathering,"

in the hopes that our friendship and fellowship
will make us men and ministers like Fuller and his friends.

I am grateful to the organizers of and attendees
at the Westminster Conference in London
and to the trustees of the Evangelical Library,
who at various times and in various ways
provided opportunities for this material
to be prepared and developed.

Contents

PART 1

Andrew Fuller's Life

1

Childhood
and Conversion

The year is 1815, and two men are dining together. One is a younger man named John Greene, the other is the celebrated preacher-orator, Robert Hall, Jr. They are reminiscing about a recently deceased friend. "Do you remember, sir," Hall asked Greene, "what occurred at his birth?" The younger man had nothing to offer. "Why, sir," Hall told him, "the fen-ditches were all convulsed, the earth shook to its very centre, and the devils ran frightened to one corner of hell."[1]

A slightly less melodramatic yet no less positive assessment comes from Charles Spurgeon, who wrote in this way to our subject's son, who was the editor of his works and author of a sketch of his life and career:

[1] John Greene, *Reminiscences of the Rev. Robert Hall, A.M.* in Gregory Olinthus and Joseph Belcher, eds., *The Works of the Rev. Robert Hall, A.M.* (New York, NY: Harper & Brothers, 1854), 26–27, n.§.

I have long considered your father to be the greatest theologian of the century, and I do not know that your pages have made me think more highly of him as a *divine* than I had thought before. But I now see him within doors far more accurately, and see about the Christian man a soft radiance of tender love which had never been revealed to me either by former biographies or by his writings.

You have added moss to the rose, and removed some of the thorns in the process.[2]

More recently described by Michael Haykin as that rare thing, "a first-class theologian," [3] and identified by Timothy George as "the most influential Baptist theologian between John Bunyan and the present day,"[4] this man who apparently scares the devils to a corner of hell and yet sheds a soft radiance of tender love is Andrew Fuller. He was born on February 6, 1754, in the village of Wicken, Cambridgeshire, a wide place in the road in the fenlands of East Anglia in the United Kingdom.

About two and a half miles from Wicken, visible across the fields, is the larger town of Soham. There Fuller

[2] Quoted by Gilbert Laws, *Andrew Fuller: Pastor, Theologian, Ropeholder* (London: Carey Press, 1942), 127.

[3] Michael A. G. Haykin, ed., *'At the Pure Fountain of Thy Word': Andrew Fuller as an Apologist* (Carlisle: Paternoster Press, 2004), ix.

[4] Endorsement of Peter J. Morden, *Offering Christ to the World: Andrew Fuller (1754–1815) and the Revival of Eighteenth Century Particular Baptist Life* (Carlisle: Paternoster, 2003).

attended church with his parents—Dissenters by birth, Baptists by conviction —under Pastor John Eve, a hyper-Calvinist. The Fuller family moved to Soham when Fuller was seven years old.

Hyper-Calvinism (or high Calvinism) of the Eve variety had brought Baptist churches to a low ebb. One element of the high Calvinist system was the insistence that the Scriptures invite only those sinners who are properly aware of their sin to turn to Christ. As a result, sinners were not warned or entreated from the pulpits to flee to the Savior, with obvious consequences.

Looking back, Fuller could say that "I therefore never considered myself as any way concerned in what I heard from the pulpit." [5] He eventually came to give this assessment: "Till of late, I conceive, there was such a portion of erroneous *doctrine* and false religion among us, that if we had carried matters a little further, we [the Baptists] should have been a very dunghill in society."[6]

---

[5] Andrew Fuller, *Complete Works*, ed. Andrew Gunton Fuller (Harrisonburg, VA: Sprinkle, 1988), 1:2. In addition to the three-volume Sprinkle edition, the Banner of Truth publishes a cheaper single-volume edition (2007). It is fair to say that none of these are pocket-sized volumes. In notes following, short references to the Sprinkle edition are to *Works*, while any short references to the more recent critical edition are to *Complete Works*, with the relevant volume identified.

[6] *Works*, 3:478.

But this is to get ahead of ourselves, for this hyper-Calvinism was the atmosphere in and doctrine under which Fuller grew up, in an environment and a community where softness could not thrive and hard work was a necessary virtue. This upbringing contributed much to Fuller's constitution and character. For example, he once said to a friend:

> My father was a farmer, and in my younger days it was one great boast among the ploughmen that they could plough a straight line *across* the furrows or ridges of field. I thought I could do this just as well as any of them. One day, I saw such a line, which had just been drawn, and I thought, "Now I have it." Accordingly, I laid hold of the plough, and, putting one of the horses into the furrow which had been made, I resolved to keep him walking in it, and thus secure a parallel line. By and by, however, I observed that there were what might be called wriggles in this furrow; and, when I came to *them*, they turned out to be *larger* in mine than in the original. On perceiving this, I threw the plough aside, and determined *never to be an imitator.*[7]

This intensity and vigor seems typical of Fuller throughout his life. He was a headstrong young man. Lying, cursing, and swearing became particular habits, though rarely without fear, for as the lad grew, he began to

[7] *Works*, 1:111.

experience powerful convictions of sin. Once, for example, singing profane songs with other boys around a smith's fire, he was struck by the thought of the words, "What doest thou here, Elijah!"[8] and left immediately, though angered with God that the Lord would not let him alone to enjoy his sinful pleasures.

From the age of about fourteen, Fuller experienced a spiritual rollercoaster ride which left him thoroughly queasy. At times, while reading Bunyan's *Grace Abounding* or *The Pilgrim's Progress* or some of Ralph Erskine's *Gospel Sonnets*, he would come under intense impressions of the sinfulness of sin, making determinations to leave it. But within days, even hours, he would return to his old ways like a dog to its vomit. Some of these feelings would have been considered among the high Calvinists as evidences of grace at work, but Fuller concluded later that the lack of fruit revealed that "the great deeps of my heart's depravity had not yet been broken up, and . . . all my religion was without any abiding principle."[9]

Increasingly torn in two directions, by the time he was fifteen he was "more and more addicted to evil,"[10] a strong and athletic youth given to great risk-taking, games of chance, and dangerous sports—what we might today call

---

[8] The language is taken from 1 Kings 19:9.

[9] *Works*, 1:4.

[10] *Works*, 1:4.

an adrenaline junkie. Wrestling was a particular attraction, and it was said that, to the end of his days, Fuller looked people up and down on meeting them, giving the impression of calculating whether he could throw them. It was a habit of appraisal that some of his later theological adversaries might have taken as a warning.

Those earlier impressions had at first left Fuller suspecting that he was a converted-but-now-backsliding believer. By 1769, still living wickedly but in great fear of hell, he realized that such an assumption was an abuse of God's mercy.

Again, high Calvinists—persuaded that only convinced sinners were invited to Christ—often pursued a "warrant" to believe that a person would be accepted by Christ (that warrant was usually a great conviction of sinfulness and great mental anguish). Despite all his miseries and crippled by the system within which he was operating, Fuller was convinced he lacked such a warrant. In November 1769, Fuller walked out alone, wrestling within himself, wrestling with God:

> I was like a man drowning, looking every way for help, or rather catching for something by which he might save his life. I tried to find whether there were any hope in the divine mercy—any in the Saviour of sinners; but felt repulsed by the thought of mercy so basely abused already. In this state of mind, as I was moving slowly

on, I thought of the resolution of Job, "Though he slay me, yet will I trust in him."[11] I paused, and repeated the words over and over. Each repetition seemed to kindle a ray of hope, mixed with a determination, *if I might*, to cast my perishing soul upon the Lord Jesus Christ for salvation, to be both pardoned and purified; for I felt that I needed the one as much as the other.[12]

Coming to Christ like Esther going into the presence of Ahasuerus, he had not before realized that the only warrant he needed was Christ's invitation to come. Now at last he found true peace, and the fifteen-year-old laid aside all his old sinful pursuits.

Indeed, under the influence of godly older men, he would leave the village during the holidays to avoid the temptation to join in with the tearaways among whom he had once been so prominent. Persuaded that believer's baptism was "the primitive way," he was baptized in April 1770 and joined the Soham church under John Eve. He was sixteen years old.

[11] Job 13.15.

[12] John Ryland Jr., *The Work of Faith, the Labour of Love, and the Patience of Hope illustrated, in the Life and Death of the Reverend Andrew Fuller* (London: Button & Son, 1816), 28–29. This is taken from a letter written to Ryland by Fuller.

2

Growth in Grace

Not long after this, the church was divided by a doctrinal question, and Fuller was unwittingly in the midst of it. The young man had challenged another member who had become drunk. The drunk man had responded that he had no power to keep himself from sin. Fuller responded to this excuse robustly but was rebuffed on account of his alleged youthful naïveté. He therefore decided to consult Eve, who confirmed Fuller's approach. Although the drunkard was soon excluded from church membership, the matter was taken up as an abstract question as to whether someone had the power to do the will of God and keep themselves from sin.

Fuller sided first with Pastor Eve and then drifted back toward the more consistent hyper-Calvinists who claimed that men (presumably, even converted men) could not keep themselves from sin. In October 1771, Pastor Eve resigned from his charge. Though never looking back on this period without grief, Fuller recognized that these contentions sent him to his Bible to read, think, and pray in ways he had not found necessary before. These wrestlings with Scripture planted the seeds that subsequently flowered in his mature understanding of God's grace at work.

But Eve's departure prompted further developments. After he left, the preaching of the Word was undertaken largely by an older man called Joseph Diver (d. 1780) who had been baptized at the same time as Fuller and had become one of his closest friends. One Saturday in November 1771, Fuller was privately pondering a passage of Scripture.

The following morning, as he made his way to the meeting place, he received a message from Diver: "Brother Diver has by accident sprained his ancle, and cannot be at meeting to-day; and he wishes me to say to you, that he hopes the Lord will be with *you*."[13] The Lord helped him, and he was asked to speak again. On this second occasion he did so badly—at least, in his own eyes—that he subsequently avoided efforts to persuade him to engage in public speaking for a year. He later lamented that he spent the years from 1771 to 1774 "to so little purpose,"[14] without the kind of investment and mentoring that might have profited him.

[13] Ryland, *Fuller*, 47.
[14] Ryland, *Fuller*, 49.

Nevertheless, Fuller's spiritual gifts became increasingly evident, and he was called by the church to preach the gospel at the end of 1774, subsequently called as pastor in January 1775, and ordained in the church on May 3, 1775 (the same year that the church joined the Northamptonshire Association). Robert Hall Sr. (1728–1791), minister of Arnsby, preached at Fuller's ordination and was something of a mentor to the young man.

As the pressures of preaching and pastoring increased, so Fuller spent more time studying and reading, wrestling with the questions which still perplexed him. Robert Hall Sr. recommended "Edwards on the will" to the young pastor as a means of coming to fixed conclusions about the previous controversy in the church. Unfortunately, Fuller started with the wrong Edwards[15] (he did not realize his mistake until 1777).

He read a number of different pamphlets and books. He compared John Gill (1697–1771) and John Bunyan (1628–1688) but initially came down toward the side of Gill. He also began to wade into John Owen (1616–1683) and found there a definite and distinct difference between the Calvinism of the sixteenth and seventeenth centuries and the Calvinism of the early eighteenth century that he had, to this point, largely inherited.

---

[15] He began with an Anglican Calvinist from Cambridge named Dr. John Edwards who wrote a volume called *Veritas Redux*.

Further pressure developed when, in 1776, Fuller met
John Ryland Jr. (1753–1825) and John Sutcliff (1752–
1814). Ryland was already substantially convinced of high
Calvinism's error regarding the free offer of the gospel, and
as Fuller and his friends read and studied the works of
Jonathan Edwards (1703–1758) and others, they grew
together toward greater light. These men, together with
others such as Samuel Pearce (1766–1799) and William
Carey (1761–1834), would become and remain Fuller's
closest companions. Fuller often relied heavily on Sutcliff
on practical issues, considering that he "excelled in
practical judgement."[16]

But despite these promptings from outside, it was
largely alone that Fuller struggled with these questions,
taking all things to the touchstone of God's Word. He
developed as a theologian by wrestling through issues
prayerfully with an open Bible, and these early years
helped him form many of his most deeply held convictions.
It was perhaps thinking of how such circumstances would
necessarily stir him up that he would later write to William
Carey, "I am a dull flint, you must strike me against a steel
to produce fire."[17] Being self-taught, he lacked some of the

[16] Fuller, *Works*, 1:353. The quote is from Fuller's funeral sermon for
Sutcliff.

[17] Quoted by Michael Haykin in "'A dull flint': Andrew Fuller – Rope
Holder, Critic of Hyper-Calvinism & Missionary Pioneer," accessed
April 25, 2013, http://andrewfullercenter.org/files/andrew-fuller.pdf.

finer academic disciplines; when given a doctorate in divinity by the Baptist College of Rhode Island, he remarked, "Now I must learn Latin in order to read it."[18]

On December 23, 1776, Fuller married Sarah Gardner. During 1777 and 1778 he began to draw up a treatise on the free offer of the gospel, feeling the need to come to a carefully considered and fixed opinion. Through this labor Fuller came to a final rejection of high Calvinism and drew up a corresponding defense of his own position, which he completed in its approximate final form about 1781 (see below). With his own conclusions established from Scripture and his conscience liberated, an immediate and necessary impact on his preaching followed.

Fuller had come to believe that faith in Christ is the duty of all who hear, or who have opportunity to hear, the gospel. [19] Discussing the nature of saving faith, Fuller demonstrated—to use Michael Haykin's summary—that "faith is fixed not on one's interest in being saved by Christ, but on Christ and his willingness to save all who cry to him for mercy and pardon." [20] Fuller demonstrated his contention from the Scriptures before answering objections.

[18] H. Leon McBeth, *The Baptist Heritage* (Nashville: Broadman & Holman, 1987), 182.

[19] The heading of Part 2 of Fuller's *The Gospel Worthy of All Acceptation*.

[20] Michael Haykin, *One Heart and One Soul: John Sutcliff of Olney, His Friends and His Times* (Darlington: Evangelical Press, 1994), 143.

Haykin identifies two main practical implications of Fuller's work. Firstly, "sinners have every encouragement to trust in the Lord Jesus for the salvation of their souls. They do not need to spend time dallying to see if they are among God's elect or if God is at work in their hearts by his Spirit. Moreover, they can no longer sit at ease under the sound of the gospel and excuse their unbelief by asserting that faith is the gift of God."[21]

In Fuller's language, "If faith in Christ be the duty of the ungodly, it must of course follow that every sinner, whatever be his character, is completely *warranted* to trust in the Lord Jesus for the salvation of his soul." [22] "Secondly," says Haykin, "ministers of the Word must earnestly exhort their hearers to commit themselves to Christ, and that without delay—anything less was unbiblical and contrary to the example of Christ and his apostles."[23]

I hope that these conclusions appear self-evident, yet I wonder if some Particular Baptists and other Reformed evangelicals today might fall short of their practical embrace. Do we have such confidence in the gospel that, on the one hand, we do not feel the urge to cloud it with carnal paraphernalia and, on the other, to declare it in all

---

[21] Haykin, *One Heart and One Soul*, 146.
[22] Fuller, *Works*, 2:383.
[23] Haykin, *One Heart and One Soul*, 146–47.

its simple and potent glory to sinners of all kinds in the expectation of their salvation?

With his mind and heart at rest and his tongue set free, Fuller had no particular desire to go into print. However, largely at the prompting of his friends and after ten years wrestling with the issue, he eventually did so, publishing *The Gospel Worthy of All Acceptation* in 1784.[24]

Here Fuller demonstrated that a man can be—must be—at the same time a Calvinist and a true evangelical. Such sentiments as these caught Fuller in a crossfire between high Calvinists and Arminians.

Many other Baptists, who could not accept what is still sometimes called "duty-faith," ostracized Fuller, the church he served, and his friends. Fuller was, by

[24] A second edition followed in 1801. There are substantial differences between the two editions, primarily arising from his treatment of particular redemption, but the essential issue was the same in each edition. The second edition employed language that suggested a shift toward a governmental view of the atonement. In this system, the death of Christ becomes less the punishment of a substitute in the place of his people and more a demonstration of God's moral government of the universe. I would suggest that Fuller did not abandon his commitments to a particular redemption by a penal substitutionary atonement, but the influence of certain New England theologians, following the Dutch jurist Hugo Grotius, did make itself felt in this later edition in ways that are undeniably unhelpful. Despite legitimate questions about certain language and illustrations, I believe that Fuller's commitment to Scripture kept him from error at this point, but those who followed him were not always so careful.

conviction, a Particular or Calvinistic Baptist, saying, "I do not believe everything that Calvin taught, nor any thing because he taught it; but I reckon strict Calvinism to be my own system."[25]

Some years after first publishing *The Gospel Worthy of All Acceptation*, responding by letter to a friend who had sent him two sermons delivered in 1799 by a preacher called William Wales Horne, Fuller wrote as follows:

> In calling the doctrine defended by Mr. Horne *false Calvinism* I have not miscalled it. In proof of this, I appeal to the writings of that great reformer, and of the ablest defenders of his system in later times—of all indeed who have been called Calvinists till within a hundred years. Were you to read many of Calvin's sermons, without knowing who was the author, you would be led, from the ideas you appear at present to entertain, to pronounce him an Arminian; neither would Goodwin, nor Owen, nor Charnock, nor Flavel, nor Bunyan, escape the charge. These men believed and preached the doctrines of grace; but not in such a way as to exclude exhortations to the unconverted to repent and believe in Jesus Christ. The doctrine which you call *Calvinism* (but which, in reality, is *Antinomianism*)

---

[25] Fuller, *Works*, 1:77; also found in Ryland, *Fuller*, 567. The notion of being a "strict Calvinist" should not be confused with being part of that denomination called Strict Baptist.

is as opposite to that of the Reformers, puritans, and nonconformists, as it is to that of the apostles.

We do not ask you to relinquish the doctrine of salvation by grace alone: so far from it, were you to do so we would, on that account, have no fellowship with you. We have no doubt of justification being wholly on account of the righteousness of Jesus; nor of faith, wherever it exists, being the free gift of God. . . . But we ask you to admit other principles, equally true, and equally important as they are; principles taught by the same inspired writers, and which, therefore, must be consistent with them.[26]

Fuller's diary entries from this period reveal a man of deep personal piety, strong conviction of sin, and genuine humility who had an eminent desire for holiness, ardent love for the lost, true affection for the people of God, and an abiding concern for the glory of God—a portrait borne out by various anecdotes.[27]

For example, his son speaks of a coach journey to Portsmouth, during which two evidently godless young men thought they could have some fun by asking their

---

[26] Fuller, *Works*, 3:583.

[27] Andrew Fuller, *The Complete Works of Andrew Fuller (Volume 1: The Diary of Andrew Fuller, 1780–1801)*, eds. Michael D. McMullen, Timothy D. Whelan (Berlin/Boston: De Gruyter, 2016). This provides a more complete record that the excerpts in the first volume of Fuller's *Works*.

serious companion if he were traveling to the town for the same low ends as themselves: "Mr. Fuller, lowering his ample brows, and looking the inquirer full in the face, replied in measured tones, 'Sir, I am a man that fears God.' Scarcely another word was uttered during the remainder of the journey."[28]

[28] Fuller, *Works*, 1:111.

3

The Elephant of Kettering

In October of 1782, after much soul-searching, Fuller accepted a call to pastor a church in Kettering, Northamptonshire. John Ryland remarked that some men govern nations with less care than Fuller exercised over moving from one local church to another. He was ordained as the pastor at Kettering in October 1783, where Robert Hall Sr. preached once more, this time on 2 Timothy 4.22: "The Lord Jesus Christ be with your spirit. Grace be with you. Amen."

On this occasion, as was typical of Baptist ordination at the time, Fuller delivered a personal confession of faith. Although the confession is worth reading in its entirety, Article 15 offers a clear window into his heart:

I believe it is the duty of every minister of Christ plainly and faithfully to preach the gospel to all who will hear it; and as I believe the inability of men to spiritual things to be wholly of the *moral*, and therefore of the *criminal* kind, and that it is their duty to love the Lord Jesus Christ and trust in him for salvation though they do not; I therefore believe free and solemn addresses, invitations, calls, and warnings to them to be not only *consistent*, but directly *adapted*, as means, in the hand of the Spirit of God, to bring them to Christ. I consider it as a part of my duty which I could not omit without being guilty of the blood of souls.[29]

Fuller was a pastor of the Kettering church from 1782 until his death in 1815. It should be remembered, as we consider some of the other strings to the man's bow, that for over thirty years he sought to be a faithful, active, loving pastor of Christ's flock. Even if we acknowledge suggestions that his pastoral ministry might sometimes have suffered because of his commitment to other labors, there is little evidence this was the case. Fuller considered mournfully that he never did see the kind of revival of religion he desired and for which he prayed. Nevertheless, during his pastorate the membership doubled, and over one thousand hearers were attending his ministry by its close. He had the heart of a true shepherd; one little notebook contains a list entitled "Families who attend at the Meeting, August, 1788," and includes the reminder "A Review of these may assist me in praying and preaching."

29 Ryland, *Fuller*, 106.

Fuller and his friends felt increasingly the pressure of the gospel on their souls. In April 1784, Ryland read Jonathan Edwards's extended treatment of Zechariah 8:20–22—"Thus says the LORD of hosts: 'Peoples shall yet come, inhabitants of many cities; the inhabitants of one city shall go to another, saying, "Let us continue to go and pray before the LORD, and seek the LORD of hosts. I myself will go also." Yes, many peoples and strong nations shall come to seek the LORD of hosts in Jerusalem, and to pray before the LORD'" —calling the saints to concerted prayer for the revival of true religion and the extension of Christ's kingdom. [30] Ryland's enthusiasm spread to Fuller and Sutcliff.

In June 1784, Fuller was due to preach at the annual meeting of the Northamptonshire Association Baptist churches. Traveling from Kettering to Nottingham, he met with floods so deep they came up to the saddle of his horse. Urged on by a local who knew the area and told him, "Go on, sir, you are quite safe!" Fuller arrived safely and preached on 2 Corinthians 5:7: "We walk by faith, not by sight." The impression left by his reading of the *Humble Attempt* was evident:

[30] The full title is "An Humble Attempt to Promote Explicit Agreement and Visible Union of God's People in Extraordinary Prayer for the Revival of Religion and the Advancement of Christ's Kingdom on Earth," in Jonathan Edwards, *Works* (Edinburgh: Banner of Truth, 1974), 2:278–312.

Let us take encouragement, in the present day of small things, by looking forward, and hoping for better days. Let this be attended with *earnest* and *united prayer* to him by whom Jacob must arise. A life of faith will ever be a life of prayer. O brethren, let us pray much for an outpouring of God's Spirit upon our ministers and churches, and not upon those only of our own connexion and denomination, but upon "all that in every place call upon the name of Jesus Christ our Lord, both theirs and ours."[31]

After this sermon, and urged on by Sutcliff, the association took up a monthly concert of prayer, asking,

Who can tell what the consequences of such an united effort in prayer may be! Let us plead with God the many gracious promises of his word, which relate to the future success of his gospel. He has said, "I will yet for this be enquired of by the house of Israel, to do it for them, I will increase them with men like a flock" (Ezekiel 36:37). Surely we have love enough for Zion to set apart one hour at a time, twelve times in a year, to seek her welfare.[32]

However, as life in the churches was being stirred up, Fuller faced battles in his own. On May 30, 1786, Fuller's

[31] Fuller, *Works*, 1:131.
[32] Quoted in Haykin, *One Heart and One Soul*, 164. Haykin suggests that Sutcliff himself drafted this call to prayer.

daughter, Sally, died at the age of six and a half years. This was one of several deaths close to the man at the same period but surely the most painful. It is a measure of his sensitivity of soul that within a few weeks his diary entries dry up, only a few torn leaves indicating the heart trouble of the following months. The diary does not open again until the Lord's Day of October 3, 1789:

> For above a year and a half I have written nothing. It has seemed to me that my life was not worth writing. Two or three years ago my heart began wretchedly to degenerate from God. Soon after my child Sally died, I sunk into a sad state of lukewarmness; and have felt the effects of it ever since. I feel at times a longing after the lost joys of God's salvation; but cannot recover them. I have backslidden from God; and yet I may rather be said to be habitually dejected on account of it than earnestly to repent of it. I find much hardness of heart, and a spirit of inactivity has laid hold of me. . . . [After recording some sermon preached:] These subjects have tended sometimes to make me long after that joy and peace in believing which I have heretofore found. But joy of heart is a feeling I cannot yet recover.[33]

The climb out of this period of spiritual dullness and desolation was painfully slow and difficult, but the Lord was upholding and helping his servant. Indeed, it was over

[33] Fuller, *Works*, 1:55–56.

the same period that the concert of prayer was taking hold to the extent that a new edition of *The Humble Attempt* was published. Neither was this the only development. At an association meeting on April 27, 1791, John Sutcliff preached powerfully from 1 Kings 19:10 on "Jealousy for the Lord of Hosts Illustrated"; Fuller delivered an equally pungent address on "The Pernicious Influence of Delay" from Haggai 1:2 in which he claimed that a procrastinating spirit cripples the saints.

It must be remembered that since the mid-1780s William Carey had been engaged in holy agitation concerning the question of Baptist missions to the unconverted. Momentum was slow to build, and though these two sermons had a deep influence—causing Fuller, Sutcliff, Carey and other to spend much of the night in prayerful discussion—delay in the matter of missions went on as counsels for caution prevailed.

Early the following year, 1792, Carey published his *Enquiry into the Obligations of Christians, to use Means for the Conversion of the Heathens*, a treatment of Matthew 28:18–20. At the association meeting in May 1792, Carey preached from Isaiah 54:2–3—"Enlarge the place of your tent, and let them stretch out the curtains of your dwellings; do not spare; lengthen your cords, and strengthen your stakes. For you shall expand to the right and to the left, and your descendants will inherit the nations, and make the desolate cities inhabited" —with two main divisions: that we should expect great things and attempt great things.[34] Again, the Spirit gripped the hearts of those present, but as the meetings drew to a close, the enthusiasm seemed to find no outlet, and it appeared that the whole project would again fizzle out. With a measure of desperation, Carey turned to Fuller and asked what could be done.

Fuller, impatient of delays, together with the rest of the gathering, finally appointed a day the following October to form a Baptist society for the propagation of the gospel among the heathen. Thus on October 2, 1792, what would become known as the Baptist Missionary Society was formed. These were the men to whom Carey bound himself, saying, "I will venture to go down [the spiritual gold mine of India] if you will hold the rope." Fuller was the secretary of the society until his death. Some measure of his commitment can be seen from the lengthy trips to Scotland he undertook in 1799, 1802, 1805, 1808, and 1813 to raise funds for the society.

Personal tragedy kept pace with Fuller. Between these two seminal meetings, he had gone through a further agonizing experience. His wife, Sarah (b. 1756), while pregnant with another child, had fallen prey to insanity. With occasional intervals of sweet though demanding

---

[34] Hence the famous epigram, "Expect great things from God; attempt great things for God."

clarity, she was often persuaded that Fuller was her jailor
rather than her husband. He wrote to Sarah's father:

It is true she never ceased to love her husband. "I have
had," she would say, "as tender a husband as ever
woman had; but you are not my husband!" She seemed
for the last month really to have considered me as an
impostor, who had entered the house, and taken
possession of the keys of every place, and of all that
belonged to her and her husband. Poor soul! for the last
month, as I said, this and other notions of the kind have
rendered her more miserable than I am able to describe!
She has been fully persuaded, that she was *not at* home,
but had wandered some where from it; had lost herself,
and fallen among strangers. She constantly wanted to
make her escape, on which account we were obliged to
keep the doors locked, and to take away the keys. "No,"
she would say to me, with a countenance full of
inexpressible anguish, "this is not my home, . . . you are
not my husband, . . . these are not my children. Once I
had a good home . . . and a husband who loved me . . .
and dear children . . . and kind friends, . . . but where
am I now? I am lost! I am ruined! What have I done?
Oh! what have I done? Lord, have mercy upon me!" In
this strain, she would be frequently walking up and
down, from room to room, bemoaning herself, without
a tear to relieve her, wringing her hands, first looking
upwards, then downwards, in all the attitudes of wild
despair! You may form some conception what must

have been my feelings, to have been a spectator of all this anguish, and at the same time, incapable of affording her the smallest relief.[35]

There did follow one last brief period of lucidity before a sudden final plunge into senselessness. Sarah gave birth to a daughter on August 23, 1792, and died a few hours later. The child, called Bathoni, survived less than a month. Such was the anvil upon which one of the architects of the Baptist mission was being painfully forged.

Later in 1792 Fuller published another substantial volume, begun some time in 1791, entitled *The Calvinistic and Socinian Systems Examined and Compared, as to their Moral Tendency*. This was a devastating broadside against Socinianism, a heresy rejecting the doctrine of the Trinity and specifically the deity of Christ, usually expressed as Unitarianism of some form. Those seeking a response to this error are still well-served by this book.

Early in 1793, taken up with preparations for Carey's departure, Fuller was struck with temporary partial paralysis (he thought it was "a slight paralytic stroke, probably occasioned by great fatigue, care, and much writing"[36]). Though he substantially recovered, the episode left him with a semi-permanent headache, often and

---

[35] Fuller, *Works*, 1:59–60.
[36] Letter to John Fawcett, quoted by Haykin in *One Heart and One Soul*, 230.

particularly brought on by intense study. In June of that year, after many tribulations, Carey finally sailed for India. In 1794 Fuller married again, this time to Ann Coles, the daughter of a Baptist minister.

4

Toil and Trouble

We clearly discern a man of unusual energy, unwearied diligence, and forthright determination. His favorite divine maxim was "Whatsoever thy hand findeth to do, do it with thy might" (Eccl. 9:10). When his wife graciously mentioned the burdens that they bore together, he replied, "Ah, my dear, the way for us to have any joy, is to rejoice in all our labour, and then we shall have plenty of joy." When she complained of his lack of recreation, he answered, "Oh no: all my recreation is a change of work." When she was concerned he would wear out, he would respond, "I cannot be worn out in a better cause. We must work while it is day," or with his favorite verses from Ecclesiastes.[37] History is silent as to whether the second Mrs. Fuller won prizes for patience, but one suspects she would have been well-placed for a medal if entered in

[37] Ryland, *Fuller*, 475–76.

national competition. In her testimony to Ryland, she stated:

> There was a degree of bluntness in his manner, which yet did not arise from an unsociable or churlish disposition; but from an impatience of interruption in the grand object of his pursuit. In this sense he seemed not to know his relations or nearest friends. Often when a friend or acquaintance on a journey has called, when they had exchanged a few words, he would ask, "Have you any thing more to say? (or something to that effect,) if not, I must beg to be excused;" at the same time asking them to stay, and take some refreshment if they chose. Yet you know, dear Sir, he had a heart formed for the warmest and sincerest friendship with those whose minds were congenial with his own, and who were engaged in similar pursuits, and I never knew him to be weary of their company.[38]

One gets the sense from this and other reports of a genuine affection and real cooperation between husband and wife. Other evidence suggests that Fuller was a father deeply invested in the well-being of his children, laboring prayerfully and practically for their blessing in every sphere of life.[39]

---

[38] Ryland, *Fuller*, 476.

[39] For a helpful overview of Fuller's family life, see Michael Haykin's lecture "Andrew Fuller: A Christian Father and Husband," accessed

However, Fuller's brusqueness came out at other times. On one occasion, a young preacher named F. A. Cox had preached with Fuller and was then invited to dine with him and his friends. Cox was invited to sit with Fuller at the head of the table but, being young and timid, attempted to decline. Cox reported that Fuller "knitted his brows" and, in a manner that "no one would wish to tempt a second time," said, "Come, sir, I like every man to take his proper place; what do you hesitate for?" After dinner, Sutcliff took Cox aside, and the young man admitted he had been a little hurt by Fuller's manner. Sutcliff replied, "Well, don't be disconcerted or discouraged. It is his manner; he does not mean anything unkind; he really loves you. My brother Fuller serves me just the same: he speaks, on a sudden, perhaps very harshly; but I know him, and let it pass; and he will soon be as confiding and affectionate as ever."[40] Something of the force of Fuller's character can be gauged from the fact that Cox was vividly recording those events some forty years after they occurred.

Other family pressures continued. In 1796 his eldest son, Robert, was proving unreliable to the point of not being able to take and hold any employment. After a series of misadventures, news reached Fuller that his son, aboard a vessel, had been tried for desertion and sentenced to a

April 29, 2019, http://www.sermonaudio.com/sermoninfo.asp?SID=717132311150.

[40] Haykin, *One Heart and One Soul*, 271–72.

severe punishment, under which he died. A few days later reports were received that this was all a lie. Robert eventually died off Lisbon in 1809, having begged his father's forgiveness and shown some hopes of repentance, although there was then no certainty of his having been in Christ. However, in 1845, long after Fuller's death, Robert's half-brother, Andrew Gunton Fuller, was preaching in Scotland, and a deacon in the congregation identified himself afterward as having known Robert in his last days. This man testified there was real evidence of Robert's having been genuinely converted.

Fuller did not engage much in polemics while in the pulpit but was obliged to contend for the truth out of it. He published in 1799 *The Gospel Its Own Witness*, the definitive eighteenth-century Baptist response to deism (largely an answer to Thomas Paine's *Age of Reason*). October of that year saw the death of Samuel Pearce, one of Fuller's closest friends. Before the end of the year Fuller had published a profoundly moving memoir of his friend, well worth reading by every Christian, not least by pastor-preachers. Pearce excelled as a preacher, in which calling his heavenly eloquence and burning passion earned him the nickname "the seraphic Pearce."

Illustrative of Pearce's character is the occasion in 1794 on which, when preaching at a five o'clock service one morning at the opening of a Baptist meeting house (the early hour designed to accommodate farm laborers), he seemed about to stop and then started again. Fuller later asked why his sermon was so oddly structured and discovered that a man had slipped in wearily at the end of the service, and Pearce was concerned lest this be the first and last time he should hear the gospel. Putting aside the possibility that his brother ministers would think little of his homiletical skills, he started again at the end for the sake of the one man, "With the hope of doing him good," said Pearce. "I resolved at once to forget all else, and, in despite of criticism, and the apprehension of being thought tedious, to give him a quarter of an hour."[41] Such were the men to whom Fuller was closest, and their mutual esteem of one another bears testimony to their quality of spirit.

"Seraphic" was not an adjective which anyone would have applied to Fuller himself. J. W. Morris—whose relationship with Fuller, it must be remembered, was fairly rocky—describes Fuller the preacher. Considering the ambivalence of Morris's perspective, the portrayal reads well and captures something of Fuller's pulpit solemnity and integrity:

> In entering the pulpit he studied very little decorum, and often hastened out of it with an appearance of precipitation; but while there he seldom failed to acquit himself with honour and success. His attitude, too, was sufficiently negligent. Not aware of its awkwardness, in

41 Haykin, *One Heart and One Soul*, 237–38.

the course of his delivery he would insensibly place one hand upon his breast, or behind him, and gradually twist off a button from his coat, which some of his domestics had frequent occasion to replace. This habit was in process of time much corrected, and many other protuberances were smoothed away by the improvement of his taste, and the collisions of society; but certainly in these respects he was not the exact model of an orator.

His presence in the pulpit was imposing, grave, and manly; tending to inspire awe, rather than conciliate esteem. His general aspect was lowering and cloudy, giving indications of a storm, rather than affording hopes of serenity. Yet there was nothing boisterous, loud, or declamatory; no intemperate warmth, or sallies of the passions; all was calm, pathetic, and argumentative, overcast with a kind of negligent grandeur. He was deeply impressed with his subject, and anxious to produce a similar impression on his hearers.

To an acute and vigorous understanding were united a rich and fertile imagination, an even flow of feeling, seldom rising to an ecstasy, and an awful sense of eternal realities; these, accompanied with an energetic manner of speaking, supplied every other defect, and gave to his ministry an unusual degree of interest. He could never be heard but with satisfaction: if the heart were not at all times affected, yet the judgment would be informed, and the taste gratified, by an unexpected display of some important truth, ingeniously stated, and powerfully applied. His own ideas were strong and lucid, and he had the faculty of placing them in the clearest light: if he failed to produce conviction, he was rarely deficient in evidence.[42]

By the early 1800s, Fuller was known and respected in English evangelical circles as a leading theologian. By now he embodied "strict [and Baptist] Calvinism" to such an extent in his writings that it became known as "Fullerism." His output remained prodigious. He was responsible for the circular letter of the Northamptonshire Association in 1810, a whirlwind tour of the Scriptures in which he sought to convince his readers of their desperate need of the Holy Spirit in the work of evangelism.

That year also saw the publication of his *Strictures on Sandemanianism*, which were, under God, used to break the great Welsh preacher Christmas Evans free of the hold that Sandemanianism had gotten on his soul. According to Evans, while reading this volume he "saw the *Rhinoceros* of Edinburgh beginning to give way, notwithstanding the strength and sharpness of his horn, before the *elephant* of

---

[42] John W. Morris, *Memoirs of the Life and Writings of the Rev. Andrew Fuller* (Boston: Lincoln & Edmands, 1830, repr. Forgotten Books, 2012), 68.

Kettering, and confess that faith is of a holy nature."[43] Evans confessed, "He undoubtedly subverted Sandemanianism in its main point, namely, faith taking place in the soul, without the regenerating power of the Spirit, or the Spirit imparting light to the soul, as the cause of it. The *Strictures on Sandemanianism* are the principal of Mr F's works, which evince him to be the greatest man of his age in powers of mind."[44]

But the elephant of Kettering did not have limitless strength. He suffered from a fever from April to October of 1811, being unable to preach for three months. In 1812 he was in London for the twentieth anniversary meetings of the Baptist Missionary Society. With an inherent dislike of pomp and circumstance, Fuller was not happy with the idea of the London celebrations and was, besides, deeply concerned for the future of the society. Fuller had high hopes for the ministerial usefulness of an eminently talented nephew of his, Joseph Fuller, but he died in March of 1812 only eighteen years old. Later that year Fuller made a tour of Wales, with the mission still very much on his heart. He preached to a vast outdoor congregation, but many ministers, suspicious of his doctrine, retired to the

[43] Quoted in Tim Shenton, *Christmas Evans: The Life and Times of the One-Eyed Preacher of Wales* (Darlington: Evangelical Press, 2001), 178. The main architects of Sandemanianism at the time were based in Edinburgh, hence Evans's play on words.

[44] Quoted in Shenton, *Christmas Evans*, 179.

chapel so as to avoid hearing him. It was only the reports of gospel progress in India that modified their opinions, and from that time on, Fuller's works were highly valued in South Wales.[45]

The East India Company was consistent and persistent in its assault on missions.[46] As a result, Fuller spent much of early 1813 in London, petitioning both in person and in writing for greater freedom for the missionaries. His productions are masterpieces of apologetic literature. In all this, Fuller was allied with William Wilberforce. Despite his ill-health, Wilberforce—who had the weight of half a million signatures behind him—spoke for three hours in the Commons on June 22, 1813, in support of the evangelization of India. The critical vote was eventually carried.

But time was marching on, and this band of brothers was being whittled down. Sutcliff preached his final sermon on February 27, 1814, dying on June 22nd the

---

[45] Gilbert Laws, *Andrew Fuller: Pastor, Theologian, Ropeholder* (London: Carey Press, 1942), 103.

[46] The East India Company, also called English East India Company, was an English, and later British, company formed for the purpose of maximizing trade with East and Southeast Asia and India. It was incorporated by royal charter on December 31, 1600. The company was not only a monopolistic trading body but also became heavily involved in politics. It was an effective agent of British imperialism and often wielded influence and power along the lines of vested and well-entrenched commercial and political interests.

same year. On June 28th Fuller preached his dear friend's funeral sermon but was himself unwell.

By September and October of that year, Fuller was suffering from an inflammation of the liver that left him able to preach only twice in that period. Always seeking an opportunity to improve a situation, he used the time to write a memoir of Sutcliff that was published with the funeral sermon.

His letters show his awareness of the situation: "Death has swept away all my old friends; and I seem to stand expecting to be called away soon. It matters not when, so that we be found in Christ."[47] To another correspondent he said, "Brother Sutcliff's last end was enviable: let mine be like his. Death has been making havoc of late among us. . . . Almost all my old friends are either dead or dying. Well, I have a hope that bears me up, and it is through grace. In reviewing my life I see much evil. God be merciful to me a sinner!"[48]

Three months before his death, Fuller was at his desk upwards of twelve hours a day. He maintained a massive correspondence but was becoming increasingly weak. Even now he showed a measured and deliberate approach: he never burned the candle at both ends but was always a steady worker—like Carey, a plodder. Fuller achieved his

[47] Ryland, *Fuller*, 541.
[48] Ryland, *Fuller*, 541.

goals by starting his work each day at a reasonable time, finishing at a reasonable time, and working consistently, methodically, and without wasting a moment during the appointed hours.

5

The End Draws Near

For all his labors, Fuller knew where his confidence lay. As his weakness increased, he began to dictate farewell letters. When one of his deacons expressed his confidence in the enviable prospect immediately before him, Fuller accepted the testimony but assured the man, "If I am saved, it will be by great and sovereign grace," and, says Ryland, he repeated those last words "very emphatically"—"by great and sovereign grace."[49]

He preached his last sermon on Sunday, April 2, 1815, a service followed by the Lord's Supper, from Isaiah 66:1–2:

> Thus says the Lord:
> "Heaven is My throne,
> And earth is My footstool.
> Where is the house that you will build Me?
> And where is the place of My rest?

[49] Ryland, *Fuller*, 547.

For all those things My hand has made,
And all those things exist,"
Says the Lord.
"But on this one will I look:
On him who is poor and of a contrite spirit,
And who trembles at My word."

The sermon was marked for its solemnity and earnestness. He had three points: "God's approval of poverty of spirit, or genuine humility: of contrition of spirit, or true repentance: of tenderness of spirit, or a godly shrinking from sin and temptation." [50] The preacher "'seemed absorbed in the contemplation of a crucified, risen, and exalted Redeemer.' It was an affecting scene— the pastor dying on his feet, worn out by excessive labour: the people, many of them his own children in the Lord, affectionate, anxious, and weeping for sorrow and foreboding fears."[51]

As his end approached, so his faith increased. When Ryland heard that Fuller had testified to a brother minister, "My hope is such that I am not afraid to plunge

---

[50] In R.L. Greenall, ed., *The Autobiography of the Rev. John Jenkinson, Baptist Minister of Kettering and Oakham* (Victor Hatley Memorial Series, vol. 3; Northampton, Northamptonshire: Northamptonshire Record Society, 2010), 22–23, quoted by Michael Haykin, accessed May 30, 2013, http://www.andrewfullercenter.org/blog/2013/05/andrew-full ers-final-sermon-vintage-fuller.

[51] Laws, *Andrew Fuller*, 120.

into eternity," he declared it the most characteristic expression his friend might have uttered.[52]

As the morning of Sunday, May 7, 1815, dawned, the sixty-one-year-old Fuller was grieved that he had not the strength to go and worship his God with his people. He spent his last half-hour seemingly engaged in prayer, though the only words that could be distinctly heard were, "Help me!" He died, said his friend Mr. Toller, an Independent minister, "as a penitent sinner at the foot of the cross."[53]

John Ryland fulfilled Fuller's last request of him by preaching his funeral sermon from Romans 8:10: "And if Christ is in you, the body is dead because of sin, but the Spirit is life because of righteousness." Robert Hall Jr., who gave Fuller that glowing testimony we noticed earlier, was called upon to deliver the oration, but this renowned preacher felt utterly dissatisfied with his efforts and never allowed his words to be published. Fuller's son found Hall after the burial, leaning against a mantelpiece in the home, his frame racked with uncontrollable tears. Later, Hall wrote of Fuller with typical floridity: "He had nothing feeble or indecisive in his character; but to every undertaking in which he engaged he brought all the powers of his understanding, all the energies of his heart;

---

[52] Ryland, *Fuller*, 550.
[53] Ryland, *Fuller*, 557.

and if he were less distinguished by the comprehension than the acumen and solidity of his thoughts, less eminent for the gentler graces than for stern integrity and native grandeur of mind, we have only to remember the necessary limitation of human excellence."[54]

Within a few years of Fuller's death, the Baptist Missionary Society had begun to lose some of its distinctive theology and piety, and ruptures were beginning to develop. The organization became increasingly independent of the churches and their pastors. John Ryland passed into glory in 1825, having faithfully carried the flame of thoroughly evangelical Calvinism among the Baptists for the balance of his life. It was, however, Andrew Fuller's death that stopped William Carey pining for England; the home country without his closest friend and most committed ropeholder held little attraction for the godly missionary. Carey was called home in 1834, the last of that great circle of friends to pass over the river, but at last reunited with them in the presence of their Lord and Savior.

[54] Quoted in Laws, *Andrew Fuller*, 123.

6

A Life in Review

Andrew Fuller's was a life consecrated to the service of Christ, the good of the church, and the extension of the kingdom of God. Though he did not always enjoy the sweetest frames of mind and heart, his character was marked by eminent godliness. Considered by William Wilberforce to be "the very image of a blacksmith,"[55] Fuller had no formal theological training, yet through faithful perusal of Scripture he came to be—and was appreciated as—a theological giant. Perhaps it was this that gave him his remarkable capacity for independent thought and his utter commitment to truth. As we have seen, he was able to say with sincerity, "I do not believe every thing that Calvin taught, nor anything because he

[55] Robert Isaac Wilberforce and Samuel Wilberforce, *The Life of William Wilberforce* (London: John Murray, 1839), 3:388.

taught it; but I reckon strict Calvinism to be my own system."[56]

Fuller was never a polished or sophisticated man. His son tells the story of how "one evening, having composed a tune, not remarkable for its scientific structure, he carried it for the inspection of a musical friend. 'It's in a flat key, sir,' observed his friend.—'Very likely,' replied Mr. F. in a plaintive tone, 'very likely; I was born in a flat key.'"[57] He loathed display and ostentation, evidencing a true humility. His was a genuine and sincere humanity, and he lived beset by normal doubts and fears, often wrestling with matters in the depths of his own heart. Despite his occasional periods of declension, trust in God marked his life—another of his favorite divine maxims was Proverbs 3:5–6: "Trust in the Lord with all your heart, and lean not on your own understanding; in all your ways acknowledge Him, and He shall direct your paths."

Fuller was not always the initiator of a course of action, but once his commitment was gained, his drive was unparalleled and his momentum seemingly unstoppable. His theological acumen was unsurpassed among his friends, and they recognized his preeminence in this. He clothed their convictions with biblical thinking, demonstrating that true concern for the lost and endeavor

---

[56] Ryland, *Fuller*, 567.
[57] Fuller, *Works*, 1:112.

for Christ always grow out of solid theology. He knew, too, the connection between crisp scriptural theology and devotion to the cause of Christ. As he pondered his death, he wrote to Ryland:

> We have some, who have been giving out, of late, that "If Sutcliff, and some others, had preached more of Christ, and less of Jonathan Edwards, they would have been more useful." If those who talk thus, preached Christ half as much as Jonathan Edwards did, and were half as useful as he was, their usefulness would be double what it is. It is very singular, that the Mission to the East should have originated with men of these principles; and without pretending to be a prophet, I may say, if ever it falls into the hands of men who talk in this strain, it will soon come to nothing.[58]

He was a man and a minister of tireless action and faith. Sermons on the pernicious influence of delay and walking by faith were not empty orations but living principles by which he himself was governed. He was not easily swayed by obstacles but marked by commitment, earnestness, and endeavor. He once fondly reminisced of enjoying "several pipes" in the company of Ryland's students, before offering the following counsel:

> It is of vast importance for a minister to be decidedly on the side of God, against himself as a sinner, and against

[58] Ryland, *Fuller*, 545–46.

an apostate world. Nor is it less important that he have an ardent love to Christ, and the gospel of salvation by free grace. I wish they may so believe, and feel, and preach the truth, as to find their message an important reality, influencing their own souls, and those of others. Let them beware of so preaching doctrine as to forget to declare *all* the counsel of God, all the precepts of the word. Let them equally beware of so dwelling upon the preceptive part of Scripture, as to forget the grand principles on which alone it can be carried into effect. We may contend for practical religion, and yet neglect the practice of religion.[59]

Here we see faith and life blended sweetly together, a love for the Bible as truth to be both believed and lived. His counsel to outgoing missionaries was thus:

Be very conversant with your Bibles. The company we keep, and the books we read, insensibly form us into the same likeness. I love to converse with a Christian, whose mind is imbued with the sentiments of the Scriptures. I find it advantageous to read a part of the Scriptures to myself before private prayer, and often to turn it into prayer as I read it. Do not read the Scriptures merely as preachers, in order to find a text, or something to say to the people; but read them that you may get good to your

59 Ryland, *Fuller*, 379–80.

own souls. Look at the Saviour as he walks, as he walks before you; and then point others to him. John i. 35.[60]

His was a character to demand veneration where it might not at first inspire love. Where it did inspire love (as it did among several close friends) it was of a deep and abiding sort. Gilbert Laws suggests that the best tribute to Fuller comes from his own mother, who survived her son. Informed by one of her other children that in the passing of Andrew they had lost a great man, Fuller's mother expressed her surprise. Assured that Andrew had written many books which were highly esteemed, the old lady replied, "Well, well, I don't know much about that; he never said anything to me about what people thought of them. I know that he was a good man, and a good son to me."[61]

His imperfections—and imperfections there were—are in themselves evidence of a vigorous, earnest man who lived life fully rather than merely existed, who always had something at hand, who was always entirely committed to the glory of God and the spread of the kingdom of Christ. Paul Brewster argues that the felt weight of Fuller's obligations fueled a lack of readiness to delegate certain responsibilities, contributing to his relative diversion from

[60] Ryland, *Fuller*, 258.
[61] Laws, *Andrew Fuller*, 125.

his primary family commitments (remember his wife's concerns) and local church duties. [62] But we should acknowledge that Fuller was setting out to practice what he preached, writing in one circular letter, "If we were in a proper spirit, the question with us would not so much be, What *must* I do for God? as, What *can* I do for God? A servant that heartily loves his master counts it a *privilege* to be employed by him, yea, an *honour* to be intrusted with any of his concerns." [63] The principle is sound, if the application is not always simple. If Fuller is a warning to us that we must seek to burn on rather than burn out, he is also an exhortation to us at least to burn rather than merely to splutter.

In a day of lukewarmness and spinelessness in which men applaud toothless sophistication over principled gumption, when men of God all too readily indulge in ecclesiastical politicking, Fuller shows the kind of man and the kind of ministry, the kind of theology and the kind of commitment, the kind of activity and the kind of preaching that the church needs as much as, if not more than, ever. Fuller reminds us that genuine light breeds real heat, true doctrine promotes zealous activity, and out of a lively faith comes an earnest life. He demonstrates a truly evangelical

---

[62] Paul Brewster, *Andrew Fuller: Model Pastor-Theologian* (Nashville: B&N, 2010), 161–62.

[63] Fuller, *Works*, 3:320.

Calvinism, a gospel which gives us a reason to go and something to say when we get there.

We have the same God in heaven, the same truth in our hands and hearts, and the same Spirit at work in our midst. With the same faith and humility, with the same conviction and determination, could we not accomplish something of the same labor to the glory of our sovereign Lord? Let us continue to pray—in our churches, in our homes, in our times of private devotion, in regular and extraordinary meetings for intercession—that God would work once more and would raise up such men to accomplish his glorious and gracious purposes in our needy times, men who can at once be a holy terror to vicious devils and a genuine delight to true saints.

At the heart of such a life and the core of such a character must be a whole-souled commitment to the Lord Jesus, forming a man who could face death and its outcome with a stable confidence:

> I know whom I have believed, and that he is able to keep that which I have committed to him against that day. I am a poor guilty creature; but Christ is an almighty Saviour. I have preached and written much against the *abuse* of the doctrine of grace; but that doctrine is all my salvation and all my desire. I have no other hope, than from salvation by mere sovereign, efficacious grace, through the atonement of my Lord and Saviour. With this hope, I can go into eternity with

composure. Come, Lord Jesus! come when thou wilt! Here I am; let him do with me as seemeth him good![64]

May God help us so to believe, so to speak, so to live, and—unless Christ returns first—so to die.

---

[64] Ryland, *Fuller*, 545.

PART 2

Andrew Fuller's
Pastoral Theology

7

Pastor and Preacher[65]

In preparing for the pulpit, it would be well to reflect in some such manner as this:—I am expected to preach, it may be to some hundreds of people, some of whom may have come several miles to hear; and what have I to say to them? Is it for me to sit here studying a text merely to find something to say to fill up the hour? I may do this without imparting any useful instruction, without commending myself to any man's conscience, and without winning, or even aiming to win, one soul to Christ. It is possible there may be in the audience a poor miserable creature, labouring under the load of a guilty conscience. If he depart without being told how to obtain rest for his soul, what may be the consequence? Or, it may be, some stranger may be there who has never heard the way of salvation in his

[65] The material in this chapter was originally delivered, in substantially the same form, at the Westminster Conference 2015, "The Power of God for Salvation." I am grateful to the conference committee for their readiness to invite this paper, for the opportunity to study the topic more carefully, and for its use in this context.

life. If he should depart without hearing it now, and should die before another opportunity occurs, how shall I meet him at the bar of God? Possibly some one of my constant hearers may die in the following week; and is there nothing I should wish to say to him before his departure? It may be that I myself may die before another Lord's day: this may be the last time that I shall ascend the pulpit; and have I no important testimony to leave with the people of my care?[66]

I imagine—I even hope—that words like these might make us wonder why anyone would ever step into a pulpit. At the same time, they should prompt that sense of holy obligation which characterized the apostle Paul: "For necessity is laid upon me; yes, woe is me if I do not preach the gospel" (1 Cor. 9:16). This call to sober preparation communicates some sense of the weight felt by its author, Andrew Fuller, concerning the work of the ministry.

Having read so far, Andrew Fuller (1754–1815) is no longer an unknown quantity to you, even if he were before. Perhaps you are reading because you have never known of him. Perhaps you have previously heard the name. Indeed, something of a renaissance in Fuller studies has occurred in recent years. Various popular and more scholarly works have rolled from the presses. The ongoing project to

[66] Fuller, *Works*, 1:715–16.

publish a critical edition of his works will doubtless open the field to others.[67]

We now know that Andrew Fuller is considered by many competent historians to be one of the preeminent Baptist theologians of the eighteenth century. He was in the vanguard of the recovery of the evangelical theology of the Particular Baptists, and, along with others like William Carey, John Ryland Jr., John Sutcliff, and Samuel Pearce, a key architect of and active participant in the missionary endeavors that characterized the eighteenth century and following.

As we have also seen, his personal pastoral ministry began in Soham, near Cambridge, as he wrestled out of his more hyper-Calvinistic background. From there he moved to Kettering, Northamptonshire, where alongside his other duties and opportunities he was the primary preacher and the pastor to a godly and growing congregation. Mutual patience and appreciation flowed between the man of God and the flock of God. In 1810 he was able to testify, "I have been pastor of the church which I now serve for nearly thirty years, without a single difference."[68] In all, Fuller

---

[67] Michael Haykin (ed.), *The Complete Works of Andrew Fuller* (Berlin/Boston: De Gruyter). Because this is a work in progress, and because of its relative expense, most references continue to be to the more readily available 1988 Sprinkle edition.

[68] Fuller, *Works*, 3:497.

was a pastor of the Kettering church from 1782 until his death in 1815.

In his monograph on Fuller's pastoral theology,[69] Keith Grant considers the pastoral and congregational implications of theological systems (theology from the perspective of the shepherd); the expression of ecclesiology and church order, notably, the relations of the minister, the church, and its other officers; and theological reflections on the office and functions of a pastor.[70] It is the last of these which corresponds most closely to my particular concern—Fuller's personal sense of what is involved in being a pastor and preacher and his counsels to others engaged in the work.

In assessing this, and to provide a measure of control, I will look primarily but not exclusively to the sermons addressed to pastors and churches (usually ordination sermons), to missionaries and to their receiving or sending churches, and to a short series of "Letters to a Young Minister" as well as some incidental correspondence and anecdotes.[71]

---

[69] Keith Grant, *Andrew Fuller and the Evangelical Renewal of Pastoral Theology* (Milton Keynes: Paternoster, 2013).

[70] Grant, *Andrew Fuller*, 7–8.

[71] There are thirty-one in total which fall into this category. These have, more recently, been collected and analyzed in Michael A. G. Haykin and Brian Croft with Ian H. Clary, *Being a Pastor: A Conversation*

My aim in what follows has been to let Fuller speak largely for himself, weaving together his insights in such a way as to give as seamless a flow as possible.

with Andrew Fuller (Darlington: Evangelical Press, 2019). Naturally, Fuller had much to say in these sermons about the relationship of the church to Christ, to the gospel, and to Christ's undershepherds, but that falls outside the immediate scope of this volume.

8

Key Influences

What streams fed this rich river of conviction and action? We should recognize some of those who helped and influenced Fuller in his development as man and minister. Among these, high on the list would be Robert Hall Sr., minister of Arnsby. Hall preached when Fuller was formally recognized as minister both in Soham and in Kettering. It was Hall who recommended Fuller read Jonathan Edwards, whose writings helped Fuller enormously as he wrestled with the nature of sin and the offer of the gospel to the needy.[72] Alongside Edwards, we should record the debt that Fuller owed to men like John Bunyan and John Owen, whose writings prompted him toward a more complete theology of the gospel.

Keith Grant identifies another important written source: an annotated translation by Robert Robinson of Jean Claude's *Essay on the Composition of a Sermon*. One of

---

[72] For more on this, see Chris Chun, *The Legacy of Jonathan Edwards in the Theology of Andrew Fuller* (Leiden: Brill, 2012).

Fuller's biographers says that "one of the first books that Mr. Fuller read, after entering on the ministry, and which he frequently recommended to others, was Claude's Essay on the composition of a Sermon; and to that work he acknowledged himself indebted, for any just ideas which he entertained upon the subject."[73] This weighty edition (in which the notes outweigh the text by a considerable margin) clearly had a significant influence on Fuller as a preacher.

Peers who kept pace with Fuller included such men as Sutcliff, Ryland, Pearce, and Carey. It is difficult to quantify the effect these ministerial friendships had on Fuller's growth and practice as a shepherd of souls. Such a study would be worthy of more time than we can now give it. However, it is impossible to read the sermons and letters of these men, or to consider their mutual engagement in the cause of Christ, without seeing their common concerns and motives and discerning the support and prompting they provided to each other in their shared work. For example, writing to another friend, Pearce offers the throwaway reminder, "If you did not plough in your closet, you would not reap in the pulpit."[74] Or think of the dying words of John Sutcliff to one of his students, quoted by Fuller in his memoir of his friend: "Preach as you will wish

[73] J. W. Morris, *Memoirs of the Life and Writings of the Rev. Andrew Fuller* (Lincoln & Edmands: Boston, 1830, repr. Forgotten Books, 2012), 69.
[74] Fuller, *Works*, 3:373.

you had when you come to die. It is one thing to preach, and another to do it as a dying man. . . . I have fled to Jesus: to his cross I am united. The Lord bless you, and make you a blessing!"[75]

We have a more certain glimpse into this kind of interaction in Fuller's diary. On Friday, September 30, 1785, there is an unusually lengthy entry:

Today we had a ministers' meeting at Northampton. I preached on being of *one spirit with Christ*—and heard Brother Sutcliff on *divine Sovereignty* from Romans 9 and Brother Skinner on Psalm 139, *Search me & try me.* But the best part of the day was I think in conversation. A question was put and discussed, to the following purport ... *"To what causes in ministers may much of the want of their success be imputed?"* The answer much turned upon the want of personal religion—particularly the want of close dealing with God in *closet prayer.* Jeremiah 10:21 was here referred to—"Their pastors are become *brutish*, and have not *sought* the Lord; *therefore* they shall not prosper, and their flocks shall be scattered!" Another reason assigned was, the want of reading and studying the Scriptures more as Christians, for the edification of our own souls. We are apt to study them merely to find out something *to say to others*, without living upon the truth ourselves. If we eat not the book before we deliver its contents to others, we may expect

[75] Fuller, *Works,* 1:356.

the Holy Spirit will not much accompany us. If we study the Scriptures as *Christians*, the more familiar we are with them, the more we shall feel their importance; but if otherwise, our familiarity with the word will be like that of soldiers and doctors with death, it will wear away all sense of its importance from our minds. To enforce this sentiment, Proverbs 22:17, 18 was referred to—"Apply thine *heart* to knowledge—the words of the wise will be pleasant if thou keep them within thee—they shall with all be fitted in thy lips." To this might have been added Psalm 1:2, 3.

Another reason was, our want of being emptied of *self-sufficiency*. In proportion as we lean upon our own gifts, or parts, or preparations, we slight the Holy Spirit, and no wonder that being grieved he should leave us to do our work alone! Besides, when this is the case, it is, humanly speaking *unsafe* for God to prosper us, especially those ministers of considerable abilities. Reference was had to an Ordination Sermon said to be lately preached by Mr. Booth of London to Dr. Gifford's successor from *"Take heed to thyself!"* Oh that I may remember these hints for my good![76]

At the end of the next month, Fuller notes that he rode to Northampton, where "Brother Ryland observed our need of watching against being defenders of practical

[76] Fuller, *Complete Works (Volume 1: Diary)*, 154–55.

religion *ministerially*, while we neglected it *practically*—referring to a passage in Dr. Owen on Temptation."[77] Earlier in the year, in the month of June, Fuller had been writing a circular letter to the Northamptonshire Association, eventually published as *An Enquiry into the Causes of Declension in Religion, with the Means of Revival.*[78] This letter contains much that is profitable for any Christian, pastor-preacher or not, emphasizing the need for a close walk with God. Clearly this was something of the air that Fuller breathed. These were themes that often exercised his soul.

Neither should we overlook the fact that Fuller was a tool formed by his Master under an often-heavy hammer on an often-painful anvil. He himself attested to this process: "Perhaps the greatest qualifications, the best instruction, the most useful learning, that any Christian minister can attain, without any disparagement of other kinds of learning, is that which is attained in the school of affliction; it is by this he becomes able to feel, to sympathize, and to speak a word in season to them that are weary."[79]

Fuller's theology interpreted his experience and helped to form his practice, and his experience enriched his

[77] Fuller, *Complete Works (Volume 1: Diary)*, 157–58.
[78] Fuller, *Works*, 3:318–24.
[79] Fuller, *Works* 1:391.

theology and equipped him for labor. To study his life is to see how his earnestness, urgency, and zeal in preaching are typical of his whole outlook. They reflect the pressures he felt in his own soul, the comforts he had discovered, the Rock upon which he built, the truths on which he rested.

That brings us to the one source that, among all other people and books, demands the first place. Fundamentally, Fuller was—in the best sense of the word—a biblicist. "Learn your religion from the Bible," he exhorted others. "Let that be your decisive rule."[80] He counseled outgoing missionaries more fully:

> Be very conversant with your Bibles. The company we keep, and the books we read, insensibly form us into the same likeness. I love to converse with a Christian, whose mind is imbued with the sentiments of the Scriptures. I find it advantageous to read a part of the Scriptures to myself before private prayer, and often to turn it into prayer as I read it. Do not read the Scriptures merely as preachers, in order to find a text, or something to say to the people; but read them that you may get good to your own souls. Look at the Saviour as he walks, as he walks before you; and then point others to him. John i. 35.[81]

---

[80] Fuller, *Works*, 1:483.
[81] Ryland, *Fuller*, 258.

Fuller went to Scripture for his message and models, for his modes and methods, for his manner and matter. It gave him his true independence of thought regarding men and his utter commitment to truth. There is no doubting that Fuller was a child of the Enlightenment—both the substance and the style of his productions and engagements demonstrates it. However, Nigel Wheeler offers this perspicuous insight: "Rather than a radical redefinition forged by the mysterious and powerful forces of Enlightenment thought, these men [including Fuller] were influenced, perhaps more so, by a static theological commitment rooted in biblical authority."[82]

This is why Fuller was able to say what he did about Calvinism: "I do not believe every thing that Calvin taught, nor anything because he taught it; but I reckon strict Calvinism to be my own system."[83] He was not ashamed of the label, but he was not overawed by the name. Instead, he went back to the Scriptures, striving not to be a mere follower of men. He urged those to whom he was a mentor and a model to do as he did: "Do not be content with superficial views of the gospel. Read and think for yourself on every subject. Read the Bible, not merely for texts, but

[82] Nigel D. Wheeler, "Eminent Spirituality and Eminent Usefulness: Andrew Fuller's (1754–1815) Pastoral Theology in his Ordination Sermons," (PhD diss., University of Pretoria, 2009), vii.

[83] Ryland, *Fuller*, 567.

for Scriptural knowledge. Truth attained in this way is like property—it will wear the better for having been acquired by dint of industry."[84]

Finally, we must not forget that Fuller really was a pastor. His pastoral theology smells of spiritual sheep. For Fuller, such study is never merely a theoretical construct for academic discussion but must always be applied. To do anything other than to live it out would be a travesty. For example, issues of exegesis and homiletics are never just abstract concerns of clear understanding and praiseworthy order and structure. The driving force behind such disciplines is the act of preaching to and the process of caring for men and women with undying souls. All his theology is truly pastoral, for his constant concern is the glory of God and the good of men and women. So even his polemical writings provide their own kind of inverse pastoral theology. Time and again we find him engaging his interlocutors with a mixture of grief and indignation, asking, in effect, "What hope can you offer to the lost? What help can you hold out to the saint?" That lies behind his earliest, more private productions as well as his subsequent forays into a more public forum. He sees the implications of error (and truth) for the souls of men at every point.

[84] Fuller, *Works*, 1:496.

Fuller incidentally reminds us that no theology is divorced from life: all theology has pastoral ramifications, for good or ill. We think again of that little notebook, previously mentioned, containing the list of families attending the services—he was constantly looking for assistance in his praying and preaching. I readily acknowledge that this emphasis colors my approach. In studying this topic from a man of this caliber, I am constantly concerned to learn from him—while, I hope, applying the same basic controls—to approach closer to the scriptural ideal for pastoral duty.

This brings us, then, to the specifics of Fuller's concern for the care of souls. What is the distinctive substance of Fuller's pastoral theology in its purest and most specific form? We can consider two streams: the man and the ministry.

9

The Man:
His Character and Calling

Fuller laid great emphasis where relatively little is laid
today: the character of the man of God. Training today
seems more concerned merely to develop a practical
toolbox for the gospel minister; modern pastoral theologies
tend to concentrate on more mechanical aspects of the
preacher's craft. Fuller, in keeping with the best tradition
of pastoral theology and his own stream of Particular
Baptist sensitivity, spoke first to the spiritual quality of the
man who was God's appointed instrument for bringing his
Word to bear on the hearts of others.

Individual Spiritual Vitality

Fuller repeatedly and rigorously enforced the maxim
that the life of a minister is the life of his ministry:
"Personal religion," he declared, "is of the utmost

importance to a minister."[85] Again and again he calls men back to the matter of their own standing with God and the health of their own souls, the ardor of their love for God and the vigor of their walk with God:

> I think it may be laid down as a rule, which both Scripture and experience will confirm, that eminent spirituality in a minister is usually attended with eminent usefulness. I do not mean to say our usefulness depends upon our spirituality, as an effect depends upon its cause; nor yet that it is always in proportion to it. God is a Sovereign; and frequently sees proper to convince us of it, in variously bestowing his blessing on the means of grace. But yet he is not wanting in giving encouragement to what he approves, wherever it is found. Our want of usefulness is often to be ascribed to our want of spirituality, much oftener than to our want of talents. God has frequently been known to succeed men of inferior abilities, when they have been eminent for holiness, while he has blasted others of much superior talents, when that quality has been wanting. Hundreds of ministers, who, on account of their gifts, have promised to be shining characters, have proved the reverse; and all owing to such things as pride, unwatchfulness, carnality, and levity.[86]

[85] Fuller, *Works*, 1:488.
[86] Fuller, *Works*, 1:143.

Not only is the gospel minister's own healthy spirituality vital for the effectiveness of his ministry, but it is—often by virtue of the very pressures and circumstances of that ministry—the element of his life that is most consistently assaulted and most easily neglected: "Persecutions—temptations—and false doctrines, sanctioned by fashion and the appearance of learning, have occasionally made sad havoc with the truth, and forced many a one who held it loosely, many a one who received his faith at second-hand, instead of drawing directly from the fountain, and who therefore never fully comprehended it, to give it up."[87] We should never simply assume that a gospel minister is a spiritually healthy man:

> I believe it is very common for the personal religion of a minister to be taken for granted; and this may prove a temptation to him to take it for granted too. Ministers, being wholly devoted to the service of God, are supposed to have considerable advantages for spiritual improvement. These they certainly have; and if their minds be spiritual, they may be expected to make greater proficiency in the Divine life than their brethren. But it should be remembered, that if they are not spiritual, those things which would otherwise be a help would prove a hinderance [*sic*]. If we study Divine subjects merely as ministers, they will produce no salutary effect. We may converse with the most

impressive truths, as soldiers and surgeons do with blood, till they cease to make any impression upon us. We must meditate on these things as Christians, first feeding our own souls upon them, and then imparting that which we have believed and felt to others; or, whatever good we may do to them, we shall receive none ourselves. Unless we mix faith with what we preach, as well as with what we hear, the word will not profit us.[88]

To sustain spiritual vitality, a minister must remember that he is a Christian man before he is a Christian minister: "One of the greatest temptations of a ministerial life is to handle Divine truth as ministers, rather than as Christians—for others, rather than for ourselves."[89] The preacher must not become a man who goes to the Bible simply for something to say, and so study the Scriptures as a preacher rather than as a Christian.

There is, then, no space in Fuller's pastoral theology for a ministerial professionalism that approaches the truth in an abstract and academic fashion: "The studying of Divine truth as preachers rather than as Christians, or, in other words, studying it for the sake of finding out something to say to others, without so much as thinking of profiting our own souls, is a temptation to which we are more than

[88] Fuller, *Works*, 1:501.
[89] Fuller, *Works*, 1:482.

ordinarily exposed." [90] Fuller charged a congregation calling a minister in this way: "The things which he urges upon you are equally binding upon himself. When he exhibits to you the only name given under heaven, among men, by which you can be saved, and charges you, on pain of eternal damnation, not to neglect it, remember his own soul also is at stake. And, when he exhorts and warns you, if he himself should privately pursue a contrary course, he seals his own destruction."[91]

Absolute Ministerial Integrity

Closely related to this and flowing out of it is the demand for absolute ministerial integrity and fidelity: "Faithfulness is absolutely required of a servant of Christ. You are not required to be *successful*: your Lord and Master was not very successful; but he was faithful, and so must you be."[92] The pastor-preacher must know and pursue his duty without deviation and distraction, his faith and his life properly joined, for a man filled with the Spirit will know how to behave in every department which he is called to occupy.[93] Fuller calls attention to Paul's language in 1 Thessalonians 2, which "exhibits him and his brethren as bold in proclaiming the gospel; sincere in their doctrine; acting as

[90] Fuller, *Works*, 1:142.
[91] Fuller, *Works*, 1:198.
[92] Fuller, *Works*, 1:498.
[93] Fuller, *Works*, 1:141.

in the sight of God; faithful to their trust, and to the souls of their hearers; unostentatious; gentle and affectionate; disinterested; and consistent in their deportment, not only among unbelievers, where even hypocrites will preserve appearances, but also among the people of their charge."[94]

This, for Fuller, was the very model of a Christian man and minister. He has not signed up for a life of comfort and applause: "Expectations of ease and honour are utterly unworthy of a Christian missionary." [95] Embracing his calling, a comprehensive and consistent godliness must characterize him in every sphere. For example, his investment in and character before his family must be above reproach, for "if you walk not closely with God there, you will be ill able to work for him elsewhere."[96] Remember the counsel he gave to Ryland's students:

> It is of vast importance for a minister to be decidedly on the side of God, against himself as a sinner, and against an apostate world. Nor is it less important that he have an ardent love to Christ, and the gospel of salvation by free grace. I wish they may so believe, and feel, and preach the truth, as to find their message an important reality, influencing their own souls, and those of others. Let them beware of so preaching doctrine as to forget to declare all the counsel of God,

94 Fuller, *Works*, 1:542.
95 Fuller, *Works*, 1:514.
96 Fuller, *Works*, 1:136.

all the precepts of the word. Let them equally beware of so dwelling upon the preceptive part of Scripture, as to forget the grand principles on which alone it can be carried into effect. We may contend for practical religion, and yet neglect the practice of religion.[97]

From this position of sincerity and fidelity, the gospel minister is to prosecute his holy business without fear or favor, speaking the truth to all without prevarication or compromise: "Study not to offend any man; yet keep not back important truth, even if it do offend. You must not enter the pulpit to indulge your own temper; but neither are you at liberty to indulge the humour of others. Be more concerned to commend yourself to the consciences of your people than to their good opinion."[98] So, regarding the unconverted, the preacher must hold back nothing that is needful: "However it may pain you, or offend your hearers, if you would preach the gospel as you ought to preach it— you must be faithful. . . . If you would preach the gospel as you ought to preach it, the approbation of God must be your main object. . . . He that is afraid or ashamed to preach the whole of the gospel, in all its implications and bearings, let him stand aside; he is utterly unworthy of being a soldier of Jesus Christ."[99]

97 Ryland, *Fuller*, 379–80.
98 Fuller, *Works*, 1:485–86.
99 Fuller, *Works*, 1:495.

When it comes to matters of righteousness, "Insist on every Divine truth and duty. Where interest or friendship stand in the way, it may be trying; but if you yield, the very parties to whom you yield will despise you. Speak but the truth in love, and speak the whole truth, and you will commend yourself to every man's conscience, when you can do no more." [100] We can clearly see that the longstanding peace in Fuller's relationships with his fellow-officers and congregation was not the peace of compromise.

Fuller insists on the pastor exercising his right to reprove and rebuke when circumstances demand it, tempered by awareness of the propriety of private rebuke when possible and compassion for the humanity of the responsible person. Thus, on the one hand, he urges, "'Rebuke with all authority;' but let your personal rebukes be private. To introduce them in the pulpit is unmanly, and would render you despicable."[101] On the other hand, he acknowledges that

> ministers, as well as other men, have their feelings. They love peace, and they wish to retain the friendship of their people. But if a minister tell the truth, there is great danger of his being counted an enemy, and treated as such. Faithful reproof, therefore, must be

[100] Fuller, *Works*, 1:490.
[101] Fuller, *Works*, 1:490.

self-denying work. The grand secret, I think, to render this part of our work as easy as possible, is to love the souls of the people, and to do every thing from pure good-will, and with a view to their advantage— "speaking the truth in love." The man that can be offended by such treatment, and leave his place in the house of God, can be no loss to a minister or to a congregation.[102]

The man of God is to shun favoritism, for "the great art of presiding in a church, so as to promote its welfare, is to be neutral between the members, always on the side of God and righteousness, and to let them see that, whatever your opinion may be, you really love them."[103] Likewise, the pastor should recognize that there are some hills worth dying on and others that can be surrendered without shame: "If we 'look on the things of others,' we may, in non-essentials, after speaking our minds, yield and be happy. But if we are determined to carry every point which appears to us desirable, in spite of the opinion of our brethren, though we may not always succeed, we shall invariably be despised for the attempt."[104]

All these duties are carried out with the felt weight of eternity pressing down: "My brother, be faithful, and you

102 Fuller, *Works*, 1:492–3.
103 Fuller, *Works*, 1:481.
104 Fuller, *Works*, 1:490.

shall receive a crown. If you be not, the eternal curse of God awaits you!" [105] Or again, commenting on the "faithful servant" of Matthew 25:21: "You are intrusted with a portion of his property, of the use or abuse of which, another day, you will have to render an account." [106] Ministers should be men with their eye on the eternal reward: "In proportion to the degree of fidelity with which we have discharged the trust committed to us in this world will be the honour and happiness conferred upon us in the next."[107] Gripped in this way by enduring realities, Fuller's martial charge rings out with urgency and pungency:

> "Make full proof of thy ministry." The word means thoroughly to accomplish that which you have undertaken. Such is the import of Col. iv. 17, "Say to Archippus, Take heed to the ministry which thou hast received in the Lord, that thou fulfil it." Were you to present a soldier with a sword, and bid him make full proof of it, he could not misunderstand you.[108]

Perhaps at this point we think that while such a man might obtain a measure of credibility, he is unlikely to be influenced by affection. That would be to miss a thread that has already become evident, and so entirely to misunderstand the matter.

[105] Fuller, *Works*, 1:496.
[106] Fuller, *Works*, 1:497.
[107] Fuller, *Works*, 1:500.
[108] Fuller, *Works*, 1:519–20.

Deep Pastoral Responsibility

According to Fuller, "an affectionate concern after [the people's] salvation" is "one of the most important qualifications for the ministry. True, it is not the only one. . . . But this qualification is that without which the greatest gifts, natural and acquired, are nothing as to real usefulness."[109] Indeed, with regard to all a man's labors, "If love be wanting, preaching will be in vain."[110] Fuller's son, Andrew Gunton Fuller, offered this perspective on the playing out of such convictions:

> Thus he prosecuted his pastoral and ministerial work, most grateful and joyous when he had experienced "a good time" in preaching or in prayer, and most deeply dejected when he had felt no "tenderness of heart" in conducting the public services. He was a constant visitor, especially at the houses of the poorer members of his church, and acknowledged that he gained much good from the practice. The griefs and sorrows of his people became his own, and he entered into their joys with all his heart. Knowing that the success of his work depended in no small measure upon his own spirituality, he hungered and thirsted after righteousness. Every hour of the day the care of the church was upon him. He thought but little of

---

109 Fuller, *Works*, 1:508.
110 Fuller, *Works*, 1:544.

popularity, but earnestly desired to accomplish great things for the glory of God.[111]

In all this, Christ Jesus himself is the great director and the true model. The very qualification that the Christ requires for an undershepherd is love: "[Christ] would not trust [his people] with one who did not love him. . . . But if we love Christ, we shall love his people for his sake."[112] A selfless communication of gospel truth flows through the life of such a man.

So it is love that governs the sphere and tone of counsel and, where necessary, rebuke. Fuller underlined that much good could be done in private that would not be appropriately carried out in public: "It is in our private visits that we can be free with our people, and they with us."[113] He assured pastors that

visiting is an essential part of your work, that you may become acquainted with the circumstances, the spiritual necessities of your people. They will be able to impart their feelings freely and unreservedly; and you will be able to administer the appropriate counsel to much better purpose than you possibly can from the pulpit, and with greater particularity than would be

[111] Andrew Gunton Fuller, *Men Worth Remembering: Andrew Fuller* (London: Hodder and Stoughton, 1882), 57–58.

[112] Fuller, *Works*, 1:477–78.

[113] Fuller, *Works*, 1:141.

becoming in a public address. Only let us burn while we shine. Let a savour of Christ accompany all our instructions. A minister who maintains an upright, affectionate conduct, may say almost any thing, in a way of just reproof, without giving offence.[114]

Indeed, "the great secret [of close pastoral dealing] is to mingle love with your fidelity."[115] Once more, Fuller contemplates his calling with an eschatological edge. Reflecting on the life and death of his dear friend, John Sutcliff, he commented: "The separation of a pastor and a people is a serious event. He is gone to give account of his ministry, and his account will include many things pertaining to the people of his charge."[116] The faithful pastor lives, serves, and dies with his people on his heart.

Developed Personal Ability

Such holy duties cannot be pursued and discharged lightly or carelessly: "A spiritual, diligent minister is commonly a fruitful one, and a blessing to his people."[117] The man of God must prepare himself for his work, recognizing its demands: "Of this preparation we have to speak; and it consists in prayer, and self-examination, and meditation. Your work is a course, and for this you must prepare by

---

[114] Fuller, *Works*, 1:481.
[115] Fuller, *Works*, 1:487.
[116] Fuller, *Works*, 1:349.
[117] Fuller, *Works*, 1:508.

'girding up the loins of your mind'—a fight, and you must 'put on the whole armour of God.' The work of God should not be entered upon rashly. God frequently brings his servants through a train of instructions and trials, that they may be fitted for it."[118]

Fuller insists on a faithful handling of the text, of understanding each portion of God's truth in its proper context, and of interpreting, explaining, and applying it accordingly:

> The great thing necessary for expounding the Scriptures is to enter into their true meaning. We may read them, and talk about them, again and again, without imparting any light concerning them. If the hearer, when you have done, understand no more of that part of Scripture than he did before, your labour is lost. Yet this is commonly the case with those attempts at expounding which consist of little else than comparing parallel passages, or, by the help of a Concordance, tracing the use of the same word in other places, going from text to text till both the preacher and the people are wearied and lost. This is troubling the Scriptures rather than expounding them. If I were to open a chest of oranges among my friends, and, in order to ascertain their quality, were to hold up one, and lay it down; then hold up another, and say, This is like the last; then a third, a fourth, a fifth, and so on, till

I came to the bottom of the chest, saying of each, It is like the other; of what account would it be? The company would doubtless be weary, and had much rather have tasted two or three of them.[119]

Such faithful handling requires both spiritual illumination and intellectual perspiration. On the one hand, Fuller can avow that "every Christian knows by experience that, in a spiritual frame of mind, he can understand more of the Scriptures in an hour than he can at other times, with the utmost application, in a week. It is by an unction from the Holy One that we know all things."[120] On the other, commenting on 1 Timothy 4:15–16, he assures us that "it is a shameful abuse of the doctrine of Divine influence to allege it as a reason for neglecting diligent study for the pulpit."[121] The gospel minister must sweat over his spiritual acquisitions:

Truth is a well—full of water, but deep. A mine—rich, but requiring much labour to dig up the precious ore. Such a depth is there in the word of God, that inspiration itself does not supersede the necessity of close application, Psal. xxvii. 4. We must be perpetually inquiring and searching, 1 Pet. i. 10–12. We must, "give ourselves" to the word of God and prayer. The very angels are perpetually gospel students, "desiring to

119 Fuller, *Works*, 1:712–13.
120 Fuller, *Works*, 1:713.
121 Fuller, *Works*, 1:506.

look into" the things that are revealed. Unless we labour in this way, there can be no proper food or variety in our preaching. "Meditate on these things: give thyself wholly to them." The truths of God's word are worthy of being our meat and drink. . . . Digging in these mines is very pleasant work when we can enter into them. But there are seasons when it is otherwise; and yet we must go on, though we scarcely know how; this is labour.[122]

Fuller demands an arduous personal acquisition of the truth that a man is to proclaim: "Do not be content with general truth.—Study the Scriptures minutely, and for yourself, and pray over your study. This will make it your own; and it will be doubly interesting to yourself and your people, than if you adopt it at second hand.—Read and think, not merely as a minister, but as a Christian."[123] Again, this is where genuine spiritual vitality is indispensable, knowing and delighting in the truth for oneself to be an effective herald of that truth: "Study the gospel—what it implies, what it includes, and what consequences it involves. I have heard complaints of some of our young ministers, that though they are not heteredox [*sic*], yet they are not evangelical; that though they do not propagate error, yet the grand, essential, distinguishing

---

[122] Fuller, *Works*, 1:492.
[123] Fuller, *Works*, 1:507.

truths of the gospel do not form the prevailing theme of their discourses."[124]

Beyond such a profound and detailed knowledge of the truth, "it belongs to the work of the ministry to apply truth to the circumstances and consciences of the hearers, as well as to teach it; and, in order to this, we must study men as well as things." For these twin tasks of teaching and applying, says Fuller, we need to labor in the fields of observation and experience.[125] No wonder Fuller calls on his brothers to devote themselves to their work and warns them of the consequences of neglect:

> To make full proof of your ministry, you must give yourselves continually to prayer, and the ministry of the word. "Meditate on these things, and give yourselves wholly to them;" and this to the end of your lives. Let no one imagine that he will leave his present situation fully qualified for the work. If, by prayer and a diligent application to study, you acquire such a habit of close thinking as that on entering the work it shall be your delight to prosecute it, this is all that will be expected of you. It is for the want of this habit of study that there are so many saunterers, and have been so many scandals amongst ministers.[126]

---

124 Fuller, *Works*, 1:509.
125 Fuller, *Works*, 1:492.
126 Fuller, *Works*, 1:520.

10

The Ministry:
Its Form and Structure

Fuller was persuaded that preaching is "the leading duty of a minister."[127] As we have seen, it is a work not to be undertaken lightly. Perhaps taking a cue from men like Matthew Henry and others before him, like many Puritans, Fuller made a distinction between "expounding the Scriptures" and "discoursing on Divine subjects"— preaching sermons.[128] Of the former, Fuller spoke of the value to preacher and people of regular exposition (in eighteen years, he said, he had "gone over the greater part of the Old Testament and some books in the New,"[129] a statement noteworthy both in the extent and the balance of the claim). Again, Fuller hammered home the need to understand the text in its context, to drink into the spirit of the writers by a proper reliance on the same Spirit upon

---

[127] Fuller, *Works*, 1:544.
[128] Fuller, *Works*, 1:712.
[129] Fuller, *Works*, 1:712.

whom they relied. "It is impossible," he asserted, "to enter into the sentiments of any great writer without a kindred mind." He never ceased to enforce the necessity of entering into that truth for oneself:

> You are aware that there are two main objects to be attained in the work of the Christian ministry—enlightening the minds and affecting the hearts of the people. These are the usual means by which the work of God is accomplished. Allow me to remind you that, in order to the attainment of these objects, you yourself must be under their influence. If you would enlighten others, you must be "a shining light" yourself. And if you would affect others, you yourself must feel; your own heart must "burn" with holy ardour. You must be "a burning and a shining light."[130]

However, Fuller considered sermons to be in a separate class from expositions.[131] It was not, of course, that they should be any less faithful to the text. Rather, sermons addressed particular subjects "in doctrinal and practical religion, which require to be illustrated, established, and improved; which cannot be done in an exposition." [132] Some might think that Fuller goes a little far in his absolutism at this point, but I wonder if it would do some good to preachers to ask whether an insistence on

130 Fuller, *Works*, 1:479.
131 See his discussion at 1:712–17 and 1:544.
132 Fuller, *Works*, 1:714.

sequential exposition as the be-all-and-end-all of preaching might itself risk an unhealthy absolutism. For sermons in particular, Fuller insisted that there be an internal unity of design, a sublimation of the preacher's capacities to the issuing of a single spiritual thrust to the heart of men.

Plain Style

The preacher should use the language of the Scripture in its proper place and with its proper force, not drawing its teeth. [133] "The doctrines of the Scriptures, Scripturally stated, are calculated to interest the heart, and to produce genuine evangelical obedience." [134] In such teaching, the preacher should "avoid vulgar expressions: do not affect finical [135] ones, nor words out of common use." [136] Fuller eschewed all rhetorical frippery and adornment, seeking to strike a balance between crassness and extravagance, calling for a sort of earthy directness:

> In general, I do not think a minister of Jesus Christ
> should aim at fine composition for the pulpit. We ought
> to use sound speech, and good sense; but if we aspire

[133] Fuller, *Works*, 1:104.

[134] Fuller, *Works*, 1:509.

[135] Fussy, elaborate, requiring great attention to detail. I appreciate the irony of Fuller's use of the word 'finical' in a sentence condemning words out of common use. I assume it was either common for him, or he is being deliberately difficult to make his point (see next sentence!).

[136] Fuller, *Works*, 1:724.

after great elegance of expression, or become very exact in the formation of our periods, though we may amuse and please the ears of a few, we shall not profit the many, and consequently shall not answer the great end of our ministry. Illiterate hearers may be very poor judges of preaching; yet the effect which it produces upon them is the best criterion of its real excellence.[137]

Cultivated Clarity

Then there must be a thoughtful ordering and structuring of material to achieve the stated aim. Fuller comments dismissively, even contemptuously, that "I say nothing of those preachers who profess to go into the pulpit without an errand, and to depend upon the Holy Spirit to furnish them with one at the time. I write not for them, but for such as make a point of thinking before they attempt to preach."[138] Men ought to prepare and preach with a laser focus: "In every sermon we should have an errand; and one of such importance that if it be received or complied with it will issue in eternal salvation."[139] He offers some practical counsel: "It might be of use, if, in the composition of sermons, we were to oblige ourselves to give titles to them. Many of what are called sermons would be found to

[137] Fuller, *Works*, 1:717.
[138] Fuller, *Works*, 1:715.
[139] Fuller, *Works*, 1:715.

require three or four titles to answer to their contents; which at once proves that, properly speaking, they are not sermons."[140] Once a man both feels and understands his material, "much depends, as to your being heard with pleasure and profit, on a proper discussion and management of the subject. At all events avoid a multiplying of heads and particulars. A few well-chosen thoughts, matured, proved, and improved, are abundantly more acceptable than when the whole is chopped, as it were, into mince-meat.[141]

Fuller resists the temptation to offer absolute rules for what cannot be ruled absolutely, or to call for elaboration where simplicity carries its own commendation:

But in all cases the division must be governed by the materials you have to divide. It would be absurd to explain a subject that was already as plain as you could make it, or in which there appeared no difficulties or liability to misunderstand. There are three questions I have often put to myself in thinking on a subject— What? Why ? What then? In other words—What am I going to teach? Why? or on what ground do I advance it as a truth? And what does it concern any or all of my hearers if it be true?[142]

140 Fuller, *Works*, 1:720.
141 Fuller, *Works*, 1:724.
142 Fuller, *Works*, 1:725.

Spiritual Insight

If the preacher is to accomplish this, he needs to know the soul of man and the truth of God, and he must be able to handle the latter appropriately when dealing with the former:

> It is not more necessary for a surgeon or a physician to understand the anatomy of the human body, than it is for ministers to understand what may be called the anatomy of the soul. . . . We need therefore to know the root of the disease, and the various ways in which it operates. In order to effect a cure, the knowledge of the disease is indispensable; and in order to attain to this knowledge, we must study the various symptoms by which the disorder may be distinguished. . . . Without [a knowledge of sanctified human nature], we shall be unable to trace the work of God in the soul; and unable to fan the gentle flame of Divine love in the genuine Christian, and to detect and expose the various counterfeits.[143]

In cultivating that unity of design which gives a sermon its driving point, Fuller encourages the preacher to interrogate a text, to determine the force of words and their relations to each other.[144] This variety then adorns and serves a unity of design.

[143] Fuller, *Works*, 1:480.
[144] Fuller, *Works*, 1:718–719.

Felt Truth

Fuller was more of the solemn orator than the pulpit poet, but it is clear he was an intense and passionate preacher. He warned against a flippant, casual, or unengaging approach: "You may preach even the gospel dryly. It must be preached faithfully, firmly, earnestly, affectionately. The apostle *so* spoke that many believed. Manner is a means of conveying truth. A cold manner disgraces important truth."[145] At the same time, he warned against "an *assumed earnestness*, or *forced zeal*, in the pulpit, which many weak hearers may mistake for the enjoyment of God"—such, he said, would be evident to the hearers and is simply disgusting.[146]

Such a compelling manner would be secured when a man was under the influence of the truth he proclaimed: "Cut off the reproach of *dry* doctrine, by preaching it feelingly."[147] There is an undeniable connection between the spiritual intensity of the preacher and the spiritual impact of his words on the congregation: "We must preach from the heart, or we shall seldom, if ever, produce any good in the hearts of our hearers."[148] Again, we must own the truth we proclaim: "How can we discourse on subjects

[145] Fuller, *Works*, 1:510.
[146] Fuller, *Works*, 1:137.
[147] Fuller, *Works*, 1:544.
[148] Fuller, *Works*, 1:546.

which we do not believe? If we have not tasted the grace of God, we shall feel no pleasure in proclaiming it to others." [149] Preachers must be men with "decided principles of their own," not preaching borrowed truth, for nothing of value is drawn from a void.[150] Once more, there must be this genuine emotion intimately and appropriately connected with the truth being handled:

> Affected zeal will not do. A gilded fire may shine, but it will not warm. We may smite with the hand, and stamp with the foot, and throw ourselves into violent agitations; but if we feel not, it is not likely the people will—unless, indeed, it be a feeling of disgust. But suppose there be no affectation, nor any deficiency of good and sound doctrine; yet if in our work we feel no inward satisfaction, we shall resemble a mill-stone— preparing food for others, the value of which we are unable to appreciate ourselves. Indeed, without feeling, we shall be incapable of preaching any truth or of inculcating any duty aright.[151]

Such genuine zeal will be properly cultivated as the minister enters into—we might almost say, realizes or actualizes—the nature of the transaction in which he is engaged.

[149] Fuller, *Works*, 1:517.
[150] Fuller, *Works*, 1:141.
[151] Fuller, *Works*, 1:480.

How would you feel in throwing out a rope to a drowning man, or in lighting a fire in a wilderness to attract the attention of one who was dear to you, and who was lost? How did Aaron feel during the plague, when he stood between the dead and the living? O my brother, enter into these feelings. Realize them. Let them inspire you with holy, affectionate zeal. Souls are perishing around you; and though you cannot "make an atonement for the people's sins," yet you can publish one, made by our great High Priest; and, receiving and exhibiting this atonement, you may hope to save yourself and them that hear you.[152]

Exalted Christ

As we would expect, Fuller warned against that preaching of self which consists in preaching for worldly advantage, for ease and laziness, for applause, for the gathering of a faction.[153] A man could even seem to be doing something good, but—if wrongly motivated—would still only be preaching his own name. Fuller therefore urged men to steer clear of curious speculations and private impulses and impressions and, rather, to make Christ "the leading theme" of their ministry:[154]

152 Fuller, *Works*, 1:510.
153 Fuller, *Works*, 1:502.
154 Fuller, *Works*, 1:516.

Preach Christ, or you had better be any thing than a preacher. The necessity laid on Paul was not barely to preach, but to preach Christ. "Woe unto me if I preach not the gospel!" . . . If you preach Christ, you need not fear for want of matter. His person and work are rich in fulness. Every Divine attribute is seen in him. All the types prefigure him. The prophecies point to him. Every truth bears relation to him. The law itself must be so explained and enforced as to lead to him.[155]

Fuller went on to exhort that his divinity and glorious character be exhibited, his mediation and atonement held up as the sinner's only hope, to press upon even the chief of sinners the blessings that come in embracing Christ, to preach him as the Lord and Lawgiver to his church:

The preaching of Christ will answer every end of preaching. This is the doctrine which God owns to conversion, to the leading of awakened sinners to peace, and to the comfort of true Christians. If the doctrine of the cross be no comfort to us, it is a sign we have no right to comfort. This doctrine is calculated to quicken the indolent, to draw forth every Christian grace, and to recover the backslider. This is the universal remedy for all the moral diseases of all mankind.[156]

[155] Fuller, *Works*, 1:503.
[156] Fuller, *Works*, 1:504.

Fuller saw Christ as the core of all Christian faith and life, the golden hub at the center of the wheel. It is through Christ that we enter the way and by Christ that we continue in the way. As a result, the whole spectrum of Christian instruction must be preached in its relation to Christ:

> Every sermon, more or less, should have some relation to Christ, and bear on his person or work. This is the life of all doctrine, and it will be our own fault if it is dry. Do not consider it as one subject among others, but as that which involves all others, and gives them an interest they could not otherwise possess. Preach not only the truth, but all truth, "as it is in Jesus." However ingenious our sermons may be, unless they bear on Christ, and lead the mind to Christ, we do not preach the faith of the gospel.[157]

What we need, therefore, is a close adherence to Christ in our ministerial labors, a tight orbit that keeps us around the spiritual center of gravity: "It must be our concern, as ministers, to know him; and, comparatively speaking, 'to know nothing else,' . . . and this that we may diffuse the knowledge of him to others. The glory of Christ's character is such that if he were but viewed in a true light, and not

---

[157] Fuller, *Works*, 1:516.

through the false mediums of prejudice and the love of sin, but through the mirror of the gospel, he must be loved."[158]

Why should this be so? Why such an adherence? "When Christ dwells in the heart, see what follows! This is the unction by which we know all things. And this is the doctrine which God blesses to the building of his church."[159]

Loving Heart

We have noted Fuller's affectionate concern for the flock of Christ. It is this which constrains the preacher: it governs the aim of his preaching, the plainness of his speech, the clarity he cultivates, the deliberations of his study, the earnestness with which he speaks, and the burden under which he labors, the declaration of Christ above all things. All this gushes from the pastor, carried along on a current of ardent love: "Cultivate the affectionate. Not indeed an affectation of feeling, but genuine feeling. Christ wept over sinners, and so must we. If we trifle with men, or be careless about their salvation, or deal forth damnation with an unfeeling heart, we do not preach 'as we ought.'"[160]

This Christlike heart of love tempers and governs all the man of God's dealings with the saints, publicly and

[158] Fuller, *Works*, 1:479.
[159] Fuller, *Works*, 1:505.
[160] Fuller, *Works*, 1:496.

privately: "Still your faithfulness must be tempered with love. There is such a thing as unfeeling fidelity—and preaching at people, rather than to them. Our Lord himself, who is a perfect pattern of faithfulness, and was particularly severe against the hypocritical Pharisees, yet wept over sinners, even while denouncing judgments against them. 'Speak the truth in love.'"[161]

Conclusion

With such governing principles as these, Fuller turns us away from the professionalism of the modern pastorate and the performances of the modern pulpit. He demands that we cultivate grace first and then gifts, neglecting neither but holding fast to both in their proper relation. To be a fruitful minister of God, the pastor must first be a faithful man of God. To reverse this priority is to invite disaster. To embrace it is to enter an excellent way in pursuit of a glorious end:

> Place yourself in idea, my brother, before your Lord and Master, at the last day, and anticipate the joy of receiving his approbation. This is heaven. We should not study to please men so much as to please God. If we please him, we shall please all who love him, and, as to others, they are not on any account worthy of being pleased at the expense of displeasing God. It is

[161] Fuller, *Works*, 1:499.

doubtless gratifying to receive the "Well done" of a creature; but this in some cases may arise from ignorance, in others from private friendship; and in some cases men may say, "Well done," when, in the sight of Him who judges the heart, and recognizes the springs of action, our work may be ill done. And even if we have done comparatively well, we must not rest satisfied with the approbation of our friends. Many have sat down contented with the plaudits of their hearers, spoiled and ruined. It is the "Well done" *at the last day* which we should seek, and with which only we should be satisfied. There have been young ministers, of very promising talents, who have been absolutely nursed to death with human applause, and the hopes they inspired blighted and blasted by the flattery of the weak and inconsiderate. The sound of "Well done" has been reiterated in their ears so often, that at last (poor little minds!) they have thought, Surely it *was* well done; they have inhaled the delicious draught, they have sat down to enjoy it, they have relaxed their efforts, and, after their little hour of popular applause, they have retired behind the scenes, and become of little or no account in the Christian world; and, what is worse, their spirituality has declined, and they have sunk down into a state of desertion, dispiritedness, and inactivity, as regards this world, and of uncertainty, if not of fearful forebodings, as to another. . . . My brother, you may sit down when God says, "Well done!" for then your trust will be discharged; but it is at your peril that you rest satisfied with any thing short of this. Keep that reward in view, and you will not, I trust, be unfaithful in the service of your Lord.[162]

---

[162] Fuller, *Works*, 1:499–500.